The Girls' Public Day School T[rust] 18[7]2–1972

A Centenary Review

Janet SONDHEIMER

and

P. R. BODINGTON, editors

GPDST
26 Queen Anne's Gate, London SW1H 9AN
1972

ISBN 0 903357 00 3

Edited by Janet Sondheimer and P. R. Bodington

Designed and produced for The Girls' Public Day School Trust by Ruari McLean Associates, London

Set in Monophoto Times New Roman and printed lithographically at the University Press, Oxford, by Vivian Ridler, Printer to the University

Representatives of the Council, the Schools, the Head Office staff and The Friends of the GPDST have collaborated in this Review. The Editors extend to all concerned their warmest thanks.

Grateful acknowledgements are due also to Headmistresses, members of staff and parents for the photographs on pp. 20, 30-34, 39-43, 46, 47, 57, 61, 62, 74, 75, 88, 90, 91, to the Trust Architect, Mr E. W. Bestow, p. 92, and to Jennifer Warren, Oxford High School, for the drawing on p. 25. Other photographs are reproduced by the courtesy of Douglas Elston, SE 21 (pp. 4, 95, 96); Messrs Bassano & Vandyk, the Middlesex County Times *and Niederer Studios, New Zealand (all on p. 4); the British Museum Newspaper Library (p. 8); Mottershaw Photography, Sheffield (pp. 21, 82, 83);* Guardian Newspapers Ltd *(p. 22); Photo-Reportage Ltd (pp. 35, 63-65); Pace, SE 7 (pp. 36, 37); Miss J. P. Alcock (p. 44); Commercial Studios, Ipswich (pp. 49-51, 93); H. Tempest, St Ives (pp. 52-54, 55); Allan Hurst, Nottingham (pp. 66, 67, 69); Cook Photography, Ealing (pp. 70, 71);* Portsmouth and Sunderland Newspapers Ltd *(pp. 76-78); C. J. Mills, Shepperton (pp. 80, 81);* Sheffield Newspapers Ltd *(p. 85); Photofinishers (Sheffield) Ltd (p. 86); the* Shrewsbury Chronicle *(p. 89); Noeline Kelly, Surbiton (pp. 97-100, 111); Les Kirby, SE 23 (pp. 102, 103); Dr John Bloss (pp. 104, 105, 107).*

Contents

TRUST HEADMISTRESSES' CONFERENCE 1971

Back row (*left to right*): Mrs Pritchett (Acting Head, Newcastle), Miss Reid (Bromley), Miss Hayworth (Ipswich), Miss Turner (Brighton & Hove), Miss Clarke (Portsmouth), Miss Wulff (Streatham Hill & Clapham), Miss Lewenz (Nottingham), Mrs Wiltshire (South Hampstead), Miss Chapman (Bath), Miss Kellett (Birkenhead), Miss Hunt (Acting Head, Shrewsbury), Miss Holt (Acting Head, Notting Hill & Ealing).

Front row: Mrs Warnock (Oxford), Mrs Piper (Wimbledon), Miss Cameron (Croydon), Miss Lutz (Sheffield), Miss Abraham (Blackheath), Miss Bartholomew (Norwich), Miss Glover (Sutton), Miss Ward (Belvedere, Liverpool), Mrs Bayldon (Kensington), Miss Smith (Putney), Miss Hamilton (Sydenham).

On grace term:

Miss Russell
(Newcastle)

Miss Hendry
(Notting Hill & Ealing)

Miss Crane
(Shrewsbury)

Introduction

This informal record celebrates the centenary of an educational venture whose major and continuing preoccupations we hope will emerge from the pages that follow. The cornerstone was the founders' determination to 'give united strength' to the isolated efforts then being made to improve the education of girls: the schools they founded remain girls' schools – not only for historical reasons but by present choice – and in our illustrations, as in the text, the varied activities and occupations of girls are given pride of place. The second preoccupation of the founders was with the type of education to be offered: their commitment to academic education as a valuable preparation for the citizen as well as the scholar has been honoured in its essentials by their successors, even if the forms, as our impressionistic accounts reveal, have changed to keep pace with changing circumstances and methods. The third preoccupation, which was quite simply to cast the net wide, both geographically and socially, has led through various stages to the present position (which is described in detail in the section '1972: the Trust today'): a community of direct grant schools scattered up and down the country but knit together by its central administration in London. The family likeness revealed by the 'portraits' of the schools is unmistakable, but their differing settings and traditions have imprinted each with its individual characteristics.

The sketches of the Trust and its schools as they are today are preceded by a historian's appreciation of the world into which the Trust (or rather the Company) was born, and by a condensed survey of subsequent developments. Some of the men and women who have contributed to that history are mentioned, albeit briefly, by name; this record honours them, and the countless others who have shared in the common enterprise.

We are fortunate that in 1972 we can take a smooth step forward into our second century. The Council of the Trust is proud of its schools and believes them to meet a real educational need. It is the Trust's declared intention to continue the work begun in 1872 by Maria Grey, Emily Shirreff, Lady Stanley of Alderley, and Mary Gurney.

1872

'In the midst of changes, of which the ever-recurring account is their irresistible necessity, it is impossible to welcome a New Year without many a misgiving' – so ran *The Times* leader gloomily of 1 January 1872. But it ended on a more cheerful note: 'May we be allowed to hope that the calamitous experience of the last two years has thoroughly disgusted Europe with war and revolution and that we may hail 1872 as the harbinger of a period of comparative peace and order.'

The same issue of *The Times* carried a letter from Mrs William Grey on the need for equality of educational rights for women – a theme which she had already made her own. She wrote to deplore the poor public response to the appeal, launched in 1871, for funds for Miss Buss's two schools: 'People do not care about the education of girls and do not think it worth giving money to.' She argued that a girl's education not only benefited the girl herself, but later her family when she was a wife and mother. She went on to stress a further reason for women's education. The latest census had shown that women far outnumbered men in the population: many would not marry and 'must at some period or other of their lives be entirely dependant on their own exertions for support'. She concluded her letter: 'The Princess of Wales has set an example to the public by sending fifty guineas to Miss Buss, as a mark of her deep interest in the better education of her own sex. Will none be found to follow that example? Is there no one in this, the richest city in the globe, capable of the generous ambition of connecting his or her name with a noble gift, and thereby sowing a seed which will bring forth fruit a hundred-fold?' The climate of the times, despite the work of pioneers such as Frances Mary Buss, Dorothea Beale, and Emily Davies, did not seem to be at all favourable to the cause of women's education and it was difficult to secure a platform for the theme. Even in women's magazines the subject was taboo; as Dr Cynthia White points out, 'no periodical which espoused the women's causes survived for more than a year or two'.

What did contemporary magazines consider to be the right and proper interests for a middle-class woman? Until the mid nineteenth century women's magazines tended to be for the upper classes, but in 1852 came the first 'cheap' magazine especially for women. This was *The English-woman's Domestic Magazine*, issued by Samuel Beeton monthly, price twopence. The contents were designed to provide 'a fund of practical information and advice tending to promote habits of industry and usefulness, without which no home can be rendered virtuous or happy'. Apart from advice on domestic management and cookery, there were notes on fashion and dressmaking, and also serial fiction. Apparently publications which offered this mixture of fiction, fashion, and needlework were successful and flourished. In 1872 a new sixpenny monthly appeared, *The Ladies*, which set out, in familiar terms, 'to aid a woman to be beautiful in her person, elegant in her dress and artistic in her tastes', and the editor assured readers the magazine would not neglect the 'less conspicuous but the more needful duties which fit her to take her proper place in the home as a wife and mother'. The delightful fashion plates show that dresses at this period were designed to disguise the natural human shape. The bustle was the rage, making the skirt protrude at the back; skirts were long and often trailing, and tight, 'glove fitting' corsets constricted the body. Even little girls' dresses were often very ornate and restricted freedom of movement. The child's dress in the illustration is described as made 'of black velvet, trimmed with swansdown. The jacket is open in front over the low bodice, velvet boots trimmed to correspond. Lace may be substituted in place of swansdown trimming.' But *The Ladies* was a magazine with a difference. Apart from the usual features, the editorials dealt with many of the questions especially affecting women and there was a chronicle of current news. Readers were introduced to topics such as women's suffrage; the new college for women, for which a site had been found near Cambridge, at Girton; women's employment; the findings of the Schools Enquiry Commission, and the proposed formation of a Girls' Public Day School Company by the National Union, a body founded to promote the education of women. The issue of 6 April 1872, for example, boldly states: 'The subject of middle class female education has a strong claim on public attention. The more it is considered the more deeply is this conviction felt and the weightier becomes the necessity of dealing with it without hesitation or prejudice.'

In many ways 1870 was a watershed in England; many of the great figures who had contributed so much to life and thought in the first half of Queen Victoria's reign had passed or were passing, and earlier reforms and movements were beginning to bear fruit. Certainly the decade, 1870–80, saw a considerable advance in the cause of women's education.

Already of course much essential pioneer work had been done. In 1848, Queen's College, Harley Street, had been established and amongst its first students were Frances Mary Buss and Dorothea Beale, destined to become famous headmistresses. Miss Buss said: 'Queen's College opened a new life to me, I mean intellectually. To come in contact with the minds of such men was indeed delightful, and it was a new experience to me and to most women who were fortunate enough to become students.' On 4 April 1850 Miss Buss, aged only twenty-three, opened her school, the North London Collegiate School, which set out to give girls the kind of educational opportunity which their brothers had in the established grammar schools. So successful was her venture that in 1871 she opened a second school, the Camden School. In 1863, mainly through the efforts of Emily Davies, the Cambridge Syndicate allowed girls as an experiment to take the same papers that boys took in their Local Examinations; from 1867 these examinations were permanently open to girls. Ninety girls entered in 1863; twelve years later the numbers had grown to 1,552. Miss

From The Ladies, *April 1872*

Davies said: 'The Cambridge Local Examinations were, I believe, the first English university examinations in which girls and boys were examined in the same subjects, by the same examiners, and judged by the same standard; the opening of these examinations was the first recognition by an English university of women as coming within the range of its obligations. The first step had thus been taken on the road towards the ultimate participation of women in university privileges on the same terms on which they are enjoyed by men.' Miss Davies took the next step towards this goal when in 1869 she opened her college for women at Hitchin; it was a modest beginning. The college was later incorporated under the name of Girton College and moved to Cambridge in 1873.

But perhaps the most important event in the history of girls' education was the appointment in 1864 of the Schools Enquiry Commission to survey the field of secondary education, for girls as well as for boys. This was the first time that girls' education had any national recognition. Amongst those summoned to give oral evidence were Miss Davies, Miss Buss, and Miss Beale, who had become headmistress of Cheltenham Ladies' College in 1858. The findings of the Commission published in 1868–9 ran to twenty large volumes; only a small portion related to girls, but it was nevertheless crucial. In brief, as the report put it: 'The general deficiency in girls' education is stated with the utmost confidence and with entire agreement.' The two main obstacles to improvement in girls' education were, first, as Miss Beale said, 'the tyranny of custom'. This theme ran through the reports of all the Assistant Commissioners and is summed up by James Bryce: 'The notion that women have minds as cultivable, and as well worth cultivating, as men's minds is still regarded by the ordinary British parent as an offensive, not to say, revolutionary paradox.' The second difficulty lay in the lack of endowments for girls' schools: 'It is evident that the endowments for secondary education of girls bears but an infinitesimal proportion to the similar endowments for boys.' The findings of the Commission were studied closely by all who were interested in girls' education and presented a distinct challenge.

This challenge was eagerly taken up by Maria Grey and her sister Emily Shirreff; as early as 1850 they had published two volumes, *Thoughts on Self Culture*, in which they drew attention to deficiencies in women's education – not to 'deficiencies in any particular branch of knowledge, but to its whole scope and purpose'. They now set out to achieve something positive to change this state of affairs by proposing a Union for improving the education of women of all classes. Mrs Grey sketched the plan they had in mind in a paper she read at a meeting of the Society of Arts in June 1871. Then at the congress of the Social Science Association in Leeds the following October the title and objects of the proposed Union were worked out and at a meeting in London in November it was formally constituted.

The prime intention of the Union was to be a 'national movement, embracing without distinction of creed or party, all who feel the importance to national welfare of an educated womanhood and are willing to assist bringing about so desirable a result'. Throughout Mrs Grey was

supported and assisted by her sister and by two friends, the Dowager
Lady Stanley of Alderley and Mary Gurney. Encouragement was also
given by HRH Princess Louise, who agreed to become President of the
Union.

One of the objects of the Union was to establish 'good and cheap day-
schools, for all classes above those attending the public elementary
schools'. Capital was needed to do this and as little could be expected
from public appeals for endowment, it was decided to form a Limited
Liability Company to raise the necessary funds. In June 1872 at a public
meeting in the Royal Albert Hall, under the chairmanship of Lord
Lyttelton, the scheme was launched, and many promised to take shares.
The Company started with a nominal capital of £12,000 in 2,400 shares
and was registered on 26 June 1872. The initial expenses for meetings and
the preliminary work, amounting to £67. 19s. 4d. were met by the Union,
but once established the Company was self-supporting and had its own
separate existence.

The policy of the Company from the outset was to found a school only
where there was evidence of sufficient demand and of adequate local
financial support. The first school opened at Durham House, Chelsea, in
January 1873 under 'Miss Porter, whose tried ability gives the best pro-
mise of success to the undertaking'. It started with 16 pupils. There
followed schools in Notting Hill in 1873, and in Croydon, 1874. The idea
gained ground, and at the Annual General Meeting of the Company on
19 February 1876 the Council reported that schools had been established
in Norwich, Clapham, Hackney, Nottingham, Bath, and Oxford with
a total of 521 pupils in attendance, whilst Chelsea now had 78 pupils,
Notting Hill 240, and Croydon 164.

The year 1872 saw the birth of what is now the Girls' Public Day School
Trust and is a memorable year in the history of girls' education. A leading
article in *The Ladies*, 30 November 1872, drew attention to the new venture: 'Those who are desirous of seeing the flimsy smattering of accom-
plishments, and the crude and parrot-like pretence of knowledge, which
passes for female education, replaced by something better, will do well to
inform themselves of the scheme I mention – a scheme which contem-
plates no disguised charity at the expense of the shareholder but a *bona
fide* investment, not one indeed to tempt the speculator, but one that
affords an opportunity of helping a good cause, with perfect security to
the capital embarked.'

In 1972 one is inclined to reflect that the investment has been worth
while.

VOICES OF 'FIRST DAY' PUPILS

*'It is not easy to realize how great was the innovation that we should be thus
all assembled together in a public school.'*

'Wasn't it a new life going to that school?'

National Union for improving the education of women of all classes

(established 1871)

The objects of the Union are stated in its prospectus:

'1. To bring into communication and co-operation all individuals and associations engaged in promoting the Education of Women and Girls, so as to strengthen and combine their efforts; to collect and register, for the use of members, information on all points connected with such education.

2. To promote the establishment of good and cheap day-schools, for all classes above those attending the public elementary schools, with boarding-houses in connection with them, when necessary, for pupils from a distance.

3. To raise the social status of female teachers by encouraging women to make teaching a profession, and to qualify themselves for it, by a sound and liberal education and by thorough training in the art of teaching; to supplement training-colleges by attaching, where possible, a class of student teachers to every large school and by such other means as may be found advisable; also to secure a test of efficiency of teachers by examinations of recognised authority and subsequent registration.

4. To extend the existing system of itinerant lecturers on special subjects, for all places not of sufficient size to maintain a permanent staff of efficient teachers.

5. To endeavour to form classes for girls in connection with grammar schools, making the teaching staff available for both.

6. To endeavour to restore to the use of girls the endowments originally intended for their benefit, and to obtain for them a fair share in the other endowments applied to education.

7. To promote the increase of the number of girls and women attending the University Local Examinations and likewise the number of centres of such examinations, and to endeavour to diminish the cost of attending them.

8. To aid all measures for extending to women the means of higher education beyond the school period; and to facilitate the preparatory and supplementary studies by forming classes for students and libraries, when

required, and enlarging the system of instruction by correspondence, already begun at Cambridge and elsewhere.

9. To assist the establishment of evening classes for young women already earning their own livelihood, and to obtain for women, when possible, admission to classes for technical instruction; thus helping them to fit themselves for better and more remunerative employments than are now accessible to them.

10. To create a sounder public opinion with regard to education itself, and the national importance of the education of women, by means of meetings, of lectures, and of the press; and thus to remove the great hindrance to its improvement, the indifference with which it is regarded by parents, and by the public.'

Teacher training and boarding

Two objects in the National Union's programme call for special comment. First the reference to the training of teachers, an activity in which the Trust at one time played a very important part. The story begins with pupil teachers and in this guise might be called pregraduate in-service training. Mrs Woodhouse, when she was at Sheffield, wrote of her students as follows: 'They are appointed as sub-helpers to mistresses capable of training them, and in large classes their help is simply invaluable. . . . Occasional lectures on method are given by specialists.' These young women were usually preparing to enter university, and to further their own studies joined the more advanced sixth-form groups. From about 1903 the greater number of the schools had Training Departments recognized by the Board of Education, in which postgraduate students were trained for secondary work and others for kindergarten or art teaching. Particular mention should be made of Clapham Training College, founded in 1900, which in addition to the three categories already mentioned also, for a short while, trained domestic science teachers. Having removed to Streatham in 1938, the college was eventually transferred to the LCC and renamed the Philippa Fawcett College, after an old girl of Clapham High School who was outstanding both as a mathematician and for her career in the Education Department of the LCC.

Kensington from 1908 to 1935 had a highly regarded department for the training of music teachers.

Second, the reference to boarding. There are now only three Trust schools with boarding houses (Bath, Brighton, Oxford – the last providing only for weekly boarders), but at an earlier stage many other schools had them, though the houses were sometimes conducted by private people, approved by the school authorities but not actually on the staff. The closure of boarding houses was largely connected with improvements in public transport, which made the need for them less urgent.

The first hundred years

The subsequent history of the Company, so vividly described in Josephine Kamm's book *Indicative Past* (published for The Friends of the Girls' Public Day School Trust in 1972) must here be presented in its barest outlines. During the first quarter century the overriding preoccupation was with the propagation and advertisement of schools, and the Company's zeal in this respect must have been conspicuous: an inquirer writing to the *Girls' Own Paper* in 1883 was directed to apply to the Secretary, A. McDowall, Esq., for 'a list of the public day schools'. The Company's own foundations – listed on page 29 – were always the result of some local initiative, insisted upon as evidence of public interest and demand. The limited liability company which originally financed these undertakings was reconstituted as The Girls' Public Day School Trust Limited in 1905, and this move led to later reorganizations by means of which the element of private financial interest was completely eliminated.

The year 1902 saw a great national advance in the provision of secondary schools, to which the Trust's schools contributed by supplying from their staffs and former pupils a large number of headmistresses and teachers. Conversely, we find pupils from state elementary schools pursuing their secondary education in schools of the Trust: the first holders of 'Technical Education Scholarships' appeared in them before 1900, and with the new century the great demand, in particular from the LCC, was for places for 'intending elementary school teachers'. These were the forerunners of the 'free placers' regularly admitted to Trust schools from 1922, when participation in a new form of general grant from the Board of Education brought schools such as the Trust's within the orbit of the state's local provision; the one-third Local Authority representation on Governing Bodies dates from that time. The condition of receiving free placers tended to reinforce the character of the schools as 'grammar schools', since these pupils were to be chosen on grounds of academic ability; and in 1923 – as it happens the year in which the Trust celebrated its golden jubilee – the Board of Education made a requirement that children from the junior schools should reach an adequate standard for promotion. The grant-aided status under which the schools now operate arose from recommendations made by the Fleming Committee in 1943.

So far the Trust has been shown as it were in its external aspect. Of its internal history – by far the most significant part of which must be traced in the records of the schools – it is difficult to speak here save in the most impressionistic terms. What follows are mere glimpses, intended to highlight some of the ways in which the Trust schools have set about 'promoting the education of women and girls'.

Interestingly enough, it is thanks to the founders' aim of increasing girls' participation in the Local Examinations conducted by universities that we are able to step inside some of those early classrooms, since the schools were also examined orally and some of the examiners' reports have survived. A set dating from 1891 shows much 'recitation' of lessons – of which some of the examiners clearly approve – and valiant attempts to teach classes 'in none of which were the girls very communicative, some being entirely silent'. The classes might also contain girls of dauntingly disparate ages (say from nine to fourteen), a circumstance due to the very novelty of the schools, which perforce had to admit quite mature girls to whom everything that happened there was Greek (Greek itself, at this date, is in evidence only at Kensington and Sheffield). The examiners show great sympathy and wisdom in their recommendations, approving whole-heartedly where they can ('I was much struck by the brightness and interest shown throughout the school') but at the same time setting the teachers the goal of achieving understanding: in chemistry, for example, it is deplored that the girls 'know the phraseology but not the logic of the subject'. Many of the headmistresses were more than capable of meeting the challenge, and in expressing their own views about what must be done show that concern for individual development which has characterized the Trust's schools. At Blackheath, for example, we find Miss Gadesden devising homework 'diaries' which if conscientiously kept should afford 'an insight into the working capacity of each pupil'. Headmistresses whose ideas were already in advance of their times, as illustrated by their requests for playing fields and by their encouragement of songs, games, and stories as ways of introducing young children to history and modern languages, must have been pleased to encounter university examiners who shared their views: thus the gentleman who insisted on provision for 'free play in concert in the open air' as a 'necessary part of the complete training of all who are young – girls as well as boys', and who looked for 'an extension of kindergarten principles up the school'. The high reputation of Trust kindergartens and junior schools was clearly established at an early date: an old girl whose school life goes back to the nineties can already speak of the 'glowing atmosphere' of her 'well-ordered' kindergarten.

The examinations which seemed so desirable to the early promoters were soon found to have their disadvantages. A speaker at the Liverpool (Belvedere) prizegiving in 1896 was already worried: 'If the new methods have annihilated all the oldfashioned objections to the higher education of women . . . are we quite satisfied that in every respect we have attained a perfect state today? One is tempted to think . . . that too many examinations are tests of book learning.' The examinations had in fact come to stay, but as ideas about the objectives and content of secondary education matured (and here women teachers in schools of all types surely played a vital part), the educational experience of the girls was doubtless enriched. The following was written of the period around 1920: 'In the sixth form the new era in teaching was already dawning; first a delicious year of general literature, and later . . . one period of general English. Then were

Miss Florence Gadesden, Headmistress of Blackheath High School 1885–1919, with some of her staff who became head-mistresses of Trust and other schools, at the Conference of the Association of Head Mistresses in 1919. *Back row (left to right)*: Miss Lewis (Wimbledon), Miss Whyte (Kettering), Miss Hopkirk (Ashby-de-la-Zouch), Miss Sanders (Sydenham), Miss Weeks (Richmond), Miss Martin (Wakefield), Miss Morant (Kentish Town), Miss Frood (Dudley), Miss Stafford (Walsall), Miss Vivian (Roundhay, Leeds). *Second row*: Miss Haig Brown (Oxford), Miss Sheldon (Sydenham), Miss Gadesden, Miss Major (Putney). *On ground*: Miss Lowe (Leeds), Miss Morrison (Francis Holland), Miss Davis (Chislehurst).

our imaginations stretched, as with faltering tongues and blushing cheeks we read aloud our heterogeneous efforts at originality.'

The twenties and thirties, one feels, brought greater cohesion to the corporate life of the schools, exemplified by the proliferation of uniforms, blazers in particular, a profusion of badges, and great enthusiasm for team games. On the work side, 'marks out of ten' were superseded by the more flexible letters, and syllabuses and curricula started to embrace new subjects such as social science, economics, and current events, while history almost spilled over into the lifetimes of those studying it (but already in 1891 the syllabus of the Oxford school ran from 1800 to 1891). The range of careers embarked upon reflect the wider opportunities created by the Sex Disqualification (Removal) Act of 1919, and also the ardent contemporary preoccupation with social conditions.

The impact of the Second World War emerges from many of the school narratives; the preservation of the Trust and its schools from extinction in such difficult circumstances was an unparalleled achievement and owes everything to the determination, resource, and loyalty of the members of the Council, officers, and headmistresses, working more than ever before as a team. That the postwar reconstruction took the shape it did was due to the Trust's decision to seek confirmation of their direct grant status for all its schools. Their share in the great upsurge towards higher and further education that followed (itself a consequence of the introduction of freely available secondary education for all under the Education Act of 1944) is reflected in outstanding successes in the new leaving examinations (O, A, and S levels), in the greatly expanded sixth forms, and in a corresponding increase in the numbers going on to colleges and universities – amongst which the new universities, with their interdisciplinary courses, exerted a particular attraction. Domestically, the fifties and sixties saw the decline of prefects and sixth-form uniform, a tendency to replace prizegivings by 'open days', and a rising emphasis on 'direct action' (Task Force and the like) to promote the social concerns which have always played an important part in the schools. As for the signs of the seventies, these must be looked for in the accounts the schools have given of themselves.

TRENDS

'*Very long black stockings, hitched up like tights, very short pleated blue serge skirts, a long woven jersey was the only uniform the school indulged in . . .*' (1892)

'*Tunics were as short as possible and girdles as low as possible and for special occasions long black stockings were sewn to knitted tights to avoid a gap known as a smile.*' (1911–21)

'*If only the corset trouble could be got over, I'm sure better (gymnastic) work could be done. What is the use of putting a nice loose tunic over a pair of corsets?*' (1908)

'*Standard light stockings became the rule, to the girls' great content.*'
(c. 1935)

'*Black stockings – in a modern phase of fashion – are unaccountably creeping back.*' (1951–61)

'*With the General Strike the modern girl seemed to materialize and I recollect the astonishing sight of a mistress being taken to an urgent appointment on the pillion of a motor cycle ridden by our first "modern girl".*' (1926)

1972

The Trust today: a 'family of schools'

The Trust's schools have not flourished in isolation. Our pleasure in reaching this centenary is all the keener in that it coincides so nearly with the centenary of the true beginnings of state education in 1870. Our schools have grown up as members of a 'great concourse', and take their place among that 'variety of schools the nation ought to have at the disposal of its children' to which we referred in our evidence to the Public Schools Commission. The Trust's schools belong specifically to those termed 'direct grant' of which there are 178, over half of them schools for girls: among the latter our schools (Kensington and the junior schools excepted) form the largest single group.

'Direct grant' schools receive grant direct from the Department of Education. The origins of the system date back to the beginning of the century; but the terms on which grant is now paid depend on regulations under the Education Act of 1944.

The regulations provide that at least 25 per cent of the entry each year must be filled by holders of free places, these places being awarded to pupils who have been educated for at least two years at a maintained or grant-aided primary school. If these places are not taken up by a Local Education Authority, they must be paid for by the Governing Body of the school. Any Local Education Authority wishing to take up places may reserve up to a further 25 per cent ('reserved places'). There must be LEA representation on the Governing Body of each school. Pupils taking the remaining places ('residuary places') pay fees, but there is provision for whole or partial remission, according to an income scale approved by the Secretary of State. Any difference between the full fees and the amount paid by parents is made up by the Department of Education. In making admissions to the schools, it is a condition that a pupil must be capable of profiting from the education there.

The Department of Education pays a capitation grant in respect of all pupils and an additional per capita grant for pupils in the sixth form.

Thanks to this system, our schools maintain close links with Local Authorities and their schools, and remain within the framework of accountability to the Department of Education. In other respects the Trust is independent, and apart from the grants already mentioned has 'to live of its own'. It is in fact entirely responsible for raising funds for capital expenditure; in this field, as the descriptions of the individual schools bear witness, the Trust owes an immeasurable debt to the generosity and enterprise of parents, pupils, and well-wishers. Among the latter must be mentioned The Friends of the Girls' Public Day School Trust, incorporated in 1952, who have made gifts to the schools, awarded travel scholarships and prizes, and whose present aim is to build up an endowment fund to mark the Trust's centenary.

But what *is* the Trust, and how does it work? The Trust as an organization is the owner of all its twenty-two senior and twenty-three junior schools, and its executive body, the Council, acts in a sense both as 'Education Authority' and 'Board of Directors', having a close knowledge of each of its schools and over-all responsibility for financial affairs. The people who work for the Trust contribute their knowledge, enthusiasm, and experience either as voluntary members or as the Trust's professional servants, and it is by their combined efforts that the daily and long-term activities of the Trust are sustained.

The Trust is fortunate to have as its Patron, in succession to the first Patron, the Princess Louise, Her Royal Highness the Duchess of Gloucester, whose interest in the schools is exemplified by the many events she has graced with her presence. The President, Dame Lucy Sutherland, is supported by a distinguished list of Vice-Presidents. The Council, which takes the main policy decisions, has a maximum of twenty members and rejoices in the inspiring leadership of Dame Kitty Anderson, the present Chairman. The Council's standing committees – Finance, Sites and Buildings, Education – are supplemented from time to time by ad hoc committees, of which a current and most important one is the Development Committee, which is reviewing development plans for the future of each school and the allocation of the money required to carry them out. Most members of Council serve on one of the committees, and some serve on most of them, devoting a considerable part of their time to the Trust's work.

The Trust's administrative officers, and the headmistresses and their staffs, are the professionals, complementing one another's work, recognizing one another's spheres. The headquarters of the Trust at No. 26 Queen Anne's Gate – an early eighteenth-century house in a street which even now preserves much of its original appearance – is the scene of constant coming and going, as committee members and headmistresses converge from all parts of the country to meet on whatever official business has brought them there, and probably to snatch a hasty but fruitful word with officers whose willing ear and ready expertise is placed so ungrudgingly at everyone's disposal. In an organization as far-flung as the Trust's, such immediacy of contact (which naturally also occurs through correspondence and telephone conversation) could not normally be assumed; that it exists exemplifies the advantages of belonging to a 'family' of schools.

There are also practical advantages. The specialized departments of the Trust's office relieve the schools of many administrative and financial responsibilities – for the collection of fees and the payment of teachers, for example, and for the structural maintenance of premises – thereby avoiding wasteful duplication of effort and resources. In these and many other fields the office staff boast an accumulated knowledge and experience on which the schools can rely.

The Assistant Secretary, the Architect (whose activities receive attention elsewhere), the Legal Adviser, the Accountant, the Surveyor – all these officers and their senior assistants carry great responsibilities. But greatest of all is the responsibility inevitably borne by the Secretary – in the person since 1952 of Mr W. Lister – who in addition to directing the multifarious activities just described is expected to act as adviser to both Council and schools, to draw Council's attention to policies needing initiation or discussion, and when necessary to speak for the Trust to the public at large.

In educational matters, the Trust's other group of professionals, the headmistresses and their staffs, are left with a free hand, subject to the general oversight of the Council. Headmistresses (themselves appointed by Council) advertise for and appoint their own staff, admit their own pupils, establish their own contacts with Local Authorities and neighbouring schools. With her staff, each headmistress is responsible for the school's curriculum, and for the school's character and good name.

In their localities the schools are greatly assisted by their Local Governors. Each school outside Greater London has its own Local Governors, of whom one third (as required by the Direct Grant Regulations) are appointed by Local Education Authorities, the rest being appointed by the Trust; a number of current governors are parents of past or present pupils, and at least one governor is always a member of the Council of the Trust. At their termly meetings the Governors receive reports from the headmistresses, consider the needs of the school and its local relationships, make representations to the Trust on these matters and are freely consulted by it. The schools within the Greater London area have similarly constituted Governing Bodies, which meet jointly.

It has been shown that the schools keep in close contact with the centre, that is with the Trust's office, and with the communities in which they live. They also maintain sporadic contact among themselves. Teams meet annually in sporting events, individuals enter for inter-school scholarships and prizes, whole forms may visit one another, whether for a picnic or for an exchange lasting several days. By this means urban girls may gain their first experience of English rural life, southerners encounter the mysterious north – and vice versa. More ambitiously still, schools combine on journeys to foreign parts: in the autumn of the centenary year Birkenhead and Liverpool, joined by representatives of nearly every other school, will set sail on the educational cruise ship SS Nevasa. On another plane, the heads of junior schools meet every year at Kensington to discuss common concerns, specialist staff gather from time to time for subject conferences, addressed by internal and external experts – a science conference will naturally include Mr A. L. Robotham, the Trust's adviser in this field – and the headmistresses confer regularly amongst themselves, as also with Council, Committees, and Local Chairmen at an annual summer gathering. In short the Trust is built on interlocking responsibilities and a diversity of personal contacts.

Personal contact plays an especially important role in the immense task of matching the schools' buildings and premises to the numerical and educational demands of 1972. The Architect and the Surveyor, not to

CROYDON HIGH SCHOOL, rebuilt 1966

mention Chairmen of the relevant committees, seem to be constantly on the move, investigating conditions on site, consulting with headmistresses, inspecting work in progress: until the day dawns when the assembled Council and a delighted school witness the opening, by the Chairman or some other important person, of a badly needed acquisition.

Building is no new preoccupation with the Trust. Most of the schools began life in large rented houses. Over the years freeholds, adjacent properties, and playing fields have been acquired, and purpose-built accommodation has been substituted or added. In a few cases, a whole school has been rebuilt on its existing site (as have the two war-damaged schools – Bath and Streatham Hill & Clapham) or has been transferred on rebuilding to a more ample site (as in the cases of Ealing, Oxford, Croydon, and, in the near future, Bromley). For almost the whole of the Trust's first hundred years, building development took place without the benefit of any income from endowments; there were no capital assets except the school premises themselves. (In this respect, the Trust has suffered from the same disability as other independent institutions for women's education – notably women's colleges.) Moreover, under the regulations covering direct grant schools, the two sources of income available, namely the grant from the central government and the fees paid for pupils (whether by Local Authorities or by parents) are controlled at a figure which, though permitting a modest surplus for repairs and maintenance, does not admit of the building up of sums for capital expenditure on improved or extended accommodation.

SHEFFIELD: church into gymnasium 1971

There are three ways in which such improvements and extensions have been financed. The first is the generosity of the schools' parents, old girls, and friends; almost every school can boast a monument to such generosity – a hall, a gymnasium, a library, accommodation for the sixth form, a teaching area, a lecture room, a swimming pool, a playing field, an adjacent property acquired. The second is by loans, the most striking example being the loan negotiated by Sir William Cash in 1959 for the purpose of improving the science facilities in a number of the schools: and it must here be set on record how greatly the Trust is indebted to Sir William Cash for all that he achieved as Chairman (from 1948 to 1964), during a period of great financial difficulty. The third is the careful channelling of such modest surpluses as were made in the whole group of schools into a building for the single school with the greatest current need. The centralized finance which makes such action possible is not the least of the benefits which the schools have gained from membership of the Trust.

But these three methods of financing acquisitions and buildings were not sufficient even to remedy such deficiencies as already existed. Still less could they meet new needs which arose from increased numbers of pupils in the sixth forms, current ideas for sixth-form facilities, or the demands for accommodation suitable for the new methods of teaching such subjects as languages and mathematics; or for new methods of learning and activity in junior schools. Nor were they sufficient for reshaping some of the schools in order to provide points of entry to fit in with new ages of

'. . . a broad educational background . . .'

transfer under local authority schemes for reorganization. It can easily be imagined, therefore, how keenly the Council of the Trust wished that there might be some annual sum which could be devoted to the improvement of school premises.

Shortly before the centenary of the Trust, this wish became a reality; for the Trust, by means of property negotiations, has acquired an income which can specifically be earmarked for building expenditure. For the first time in the history of the Trust, the Council knew that it would be able to spend a specified annual sum on the physical needs of the schools. Every effort was made to identify the most crying needs in terms, not only of deficiencies but also of the foreseeable new demands on the Trust's educational contribution within an area. Obviously these needs will take very many years to meet. But, as a start, a five-year plan for the years 1971 to 1975 was drawn up. The projects include science blocks at South Hampstead, Sutton, Nottingham, Norwich, Wimbledon, Putney, and Portsmouth and improved science facilities at Blackheath, Bath, and Newcastle; a hall or gymnasium or gym hall at Belvedere, Brighton, Newcastle, Sheffield, Shrewsbury, and Sydenham; formrooms or subject rooms at Ipswich, Bath, Norwich, Sheffield, and Sutton; facilities for art at Blackheath, Portsmouth, Birkenhead; sixth-form accommodation at Oxford and, combined with a new library, at Notting Hill & Ealing; extra rooms for the junior school at Blackheath, Ipswich, Putney, Norwich, Newcastle, and Sydenham. The joy does not end with the new buildings for, in most cases, there is a new use for liberated areas. For instance, a vacated hall may become a spacious and beautiful library, vacated laboratories may turn into formrooms or subject rooms, or into a sixth-form area; a vacated studio may become a staffroom . . . the chain reaction arising from any new building is complex and fascinating.

Many of these projects could not have been given their place in the programme without a contribution from the proceeds of Appeals launched by the schools themselves; other projects are being provided by school enterprise without financial aid from the Trust. There is no limit to the help which can still be given by the generosity of the schools' parents, old girls, and friends; for thus each five-year plan will be enabled to embrace yet more projects, as the second century of the Trust proceeds.

It is impossible to predict what changes may occur in the life lived within our buildings. That it will change is certain: the schools would not be alive today if they still adhered to the educational styles of 1872, bold as they were in their day. All we can do here is to describe, in broad outline, the work of the schools as they are now.

The schools of the Trust have by tradition a high regard for academic values and they aim at combining this with a broad educational background and a flexible adaptation of courses to meet the needs of each individual. Being small enough for personal considerations to count, yet sufficiently homogeneous to make such a scheme economically viable, they have produced an interesting amalgam which gives their academic work a distinctive character.

Knowing their reputation for academic studies, parents who choose these schools expect their daughters to be intellectually stretched and usually encourage them to work to capacity; under the guidance of able teachers, girls of varying gifts respond to the atmosphere of interest and endeavour, usually with encouraging results. Within a broadly based educational framework, girls pass up the school in unstreamed forms of mixed ability, only dividing into sets when it seems advisable to vary pace or method. Specialization is deferred as long as possible and is, at all stages, balanced by general studies. Another characteristic common to the twenty-two schools is the long span of school life. Very few pupils leave without a sixth-form course and continuity of planning is thus made possible over a period of seven years in the senior school; many, in addition, may have come through the junior department in a course continuous from the age of around five to eight. It is also characteristic that nearly all the staff teach throughout the senior school, so that the most highly qualified teachers meet the younger girls as well as the sixth forms.

The wide range of subjects offered include some which are quite unusual. In one school or another one finds, for example, Russian, Italian, British Constitution, Economic and Public Affairs, Geology, Textiles and Dress being offered as Advanced Level subjects. Sixth forms in which nearly all girls are following at least two Advanced Level courses make it possible to form sizable and stimulating teaching groups. At the same time the creative arts have a natural place both as examination and as minority subjects: in some schools music has attained an outstanding prominence. General and supporting courses are provided on a generous scale in all sixth forms, with considerable adaptation of time-tables to suit individual needs and tastes.

When the time comes to leave, the young women go on to a very diverse and extensive range of occupations. In 1970, out of a total of 1,443 leavers, 43 per cent went on to university or other degree courses, 38 per cent to colleges of education and other further education, 19 per cent to paid employment, including those professions which provide their own training. From this it will be seen that in admitting pupils, many kinds of ability and quality are recognized and encouraged, which do not necessarily lead to universities but which enrich the schools and add refreshing diversity to the later careers of school leavers.

The
Schools

The Schools past and present

The accounts which follow are of existing schools. But the centenary record should also make specific reference to the schools which have closed, or which continue their existence under other auspices, or are merged with neighbouring Trust schools. These vanished schools were and are regarded with no less affection than the rest. An old girl of York, for example, writing in 1952, describes it as 'a school struggling against odds' and continues 'but how good it was! . . . I was only fifteen when it came to an end, but the friendship of the staff went on. It is with me still.' Some of these schools enjoyed settings and buildings of quite exceptional interest: York again, which 'had the minster in the background to give perpetual dignity to life'; Highbury & Islington, lodged in early tudor Canonbury tower, with its later additions of 'wonderful plaster ceilings and beautiful Adam mantelpieces'. Tunbridge Wells opened in a house with the evocative name of Mount Sion, and as befitted a Kentish school later moved to a house with a beautiful garden. Nor should it be supposed that these schools were unprogressive: at Swansea they had a skeleton and taught hygiene – as the headmistress put it, 'the Welsh mind seems especially fitted for the study of science – we find the children look on these lessons as recreation'.

Clapham, in that it finally evolved from experiments in school organization attempted nowhere else by the Trust, stands in a class on its own; and it is partly for that reason that it is described in greater detail.

It may not be generally known that the High School was preceded in Clapham by another school called Clapham Middle School, opened by the Company in 1875, and in 1894 reorganized as the Modern School, which continued until 1904. In 1882 the Company founded the High School, with which, in 1904, the Modern School was amalgamated; from then on, the High School represented all three foundations.

It has been said that no one could be at Clapham High School for even a very short time without realizing that it was a school with a special tradition, an atmosphere all its own. That tradition it owed in a large measure to its founders and early makers, particularly the first headmistress, Miss O'Connor (one of the pioneers of the higher education of women) and her successor after sixteen years, the legendary Mrs Woodhouse, who for fourteen years directed, consolidated, expanded, and inspired the work of the school. But throughout its history until its unavoidable but much-regretted closure in 1938, Clapham was fortunate in having only the finest of headmistresses, together with a teaching staff of exceptional quality and dedication.

The training and education received at Clapham High School was of the highest possible standard, and the results of this are shown in the long list of old girls who have won distinction for themselves and the school in so many fields. One of these is remembered with particular pride and affection: Lilian Charlesworth, who gave such outstanding service as a Trust headmistress for twenty-eight years.

The school was situated in a fine position on South Side, Clapham Common; an imposing building, with a delightful garden at the rear – all old girls remember the lawn with the cedar tree! Inside, the assembly hall with its lovely organ and polished teak floor was most impressive; the classrooms were large and airy, but those at the front of the building had double windows to minimize the noise from the traffic in the main road. The junior school was in a separate building, Elms House, a few yards along the road.

The arts were specially encouraged at Clapham, and the well-equipped studio was a delight. Music in all its forms, but particularly singing, was considered a vital and essential part of the curriculum, and was extremely well taught. Physical education was also most important, with a fine gymnasium, netball courts, and fives courts on the premises.

There was always a strong link with the UGS Mission, and the Settlement was well supported in many ways by the Clapham girls; this support continues today through the Old Girls' Society, which still flourishes in spite of there being no school to provide new members. Its Annual Meeting is always well attended, and although, naturally, many of its members are now elderly, all keep in touch thanks to an admirable News Letter and an unquenchable affection for the old school.

As Miss Jarrett wrote in the last number of the Clapham magazine: 'We have, indeed, so much to be thankful for in all that Clapham High School has stood for in its great contribution to education, and in the many great personalities who shaped its destiny and enriched its history.'

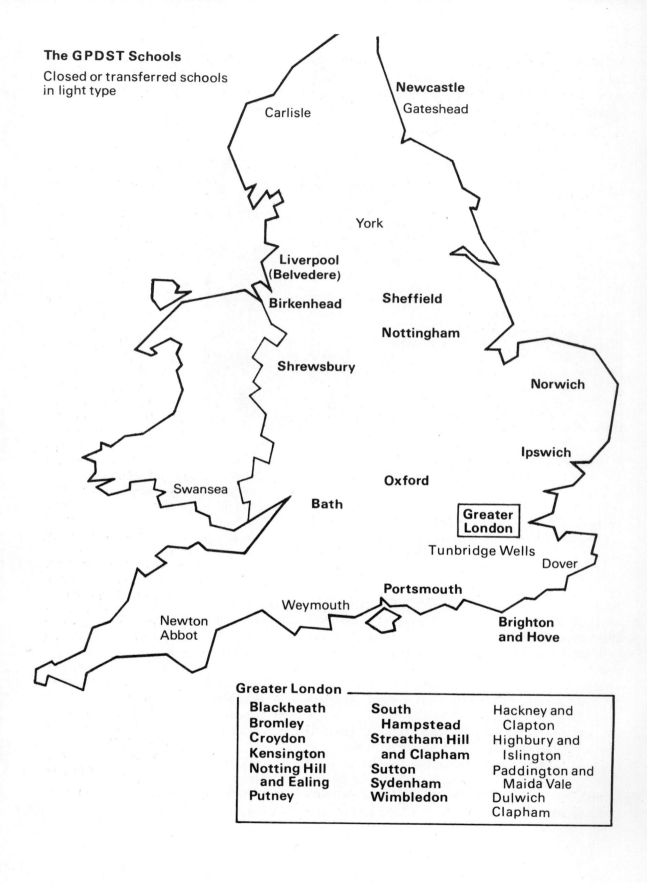

The GPDST Schools

Closed or transferred schools in light type

Carlisle

Newcastle
Gateshead

York

Liverpool
(Belvedere)

Birkenhead

Sheffield

Nottingham

Shrewsbury

Norwich

Ipswich

Swansea

Bath

Oxford

Greater
London

Tunbridge Wells

Dover

Portsmouth

Newton
Abbot

Weymouth

Brighton
and Hove

Greater London

Blackheath	**South**	Hackney and
Bromley	**Hampstead**	Clapton
Croydon	**Streatham Hill**	Highbury and
Kensington	**and Clapham**	Islington
Notting Hill	**Sutton**	Paddington and
and Ealing	**Sydenham**	Maida Vale
Putney	**Wimbledon**	Dulwich
		Clapham

The Schools in order of foundation and their first Headmistresses

1873	KENSINGTON (originally CHELSEA)	MISS M. E. PORTER
	NOTTING HILL & BAYSWATER (now NOTTING HILL & EALING)	MISS H. M. JONES
1874	CROYDON	MISS D. NELIGAN
1875	NORWICH	MISS A. BENSON
	HACKNEY (subsequently CLAPTON) – closed 1899	MISS M. PEARSE
	CLAPHAM (MIDDLE-MODERN) – merged 1904 with CLAPHAM HIGH	MISS M. A. ALGER
	NOTTINGHAM	MRS C. F. BOLTON
	BATH	MISS S. WOOD
	OXFORD	MISS A. BENSON
1876	SOUTH HAMPSTEAD (originally ST JOHN'S WOOD)	MISS R. ALLEN-OLNEY
	BRIGHTON (now BRIGHTON & HOVE)	MISS E. E. M. CREAK
	GATESHEAD – merged 1907 with NEWCASTLE	MISS J. P. ROWDON
1878	HIGHBURY & ISLINGTON – closed 1911	MISS M. C. WHYTE
	MAIDA VALE (later PADDINGTON & MAIDA VALE) – transferred 1912 to LCC	MISS A. C. ANDREWS
	SHEFFIELD	MISS M. A. ALGER
	IPSWICH	MISS S. E. YOUNGMAN
	DULWICH – transferred 1913 to Church Schools Company, closed 1938	MISS M. A. ALGER
1880	BLACKHEATH	MISS S. ALLEN-OLNEY
	LIVERPOOL (now BELVEDERE)	MRS C. F. BOLTON
	WEYMOUTH – closed 1894	MISS F. K. FIRTH
	YORK – transferred 1907 to Church Schools Company, now York College for Girls	MISS E. K. W. CHAMBERS
	WIMBLEDON	MISS E. M. HASTINGS
1881	NEWTON ABBOT – became a private school 1888	MISS L. GADESDEN
1882	PORTSMOUTH	MISS A. LEDGER
	CLAPHAM (HIGH) – merged 1938 with STREATHAM HILL & BRIXTON	MISS A. A. O'CONNOR
1883	BROMLEY	MISS M. L. HEPPEL
	TUNBRIDGE WELLS – closed 1945	MISS M. MOBERLY
1884	CARLISLE – transferred 1909 to Cumberland County Council	MISS I. BAIN
	SUTTON	MISS M. C. WHYTE
1885	SHREWSBURY	MISS E. CANNINGS
1887	STREATHAM HILL & BRIXTON (originally BRIXTON HILL) – now STREATHAM HILL & CLAPHAM	MISS A. TOVEY
	SYDENHAM	MISS I. THOMAS
1888	DOVER – closed 1908	MISS G. E. FROST
	SWANSEA – closed 1895	MISS M. E. VINTER
1891	EAST LIVERPOOL – merged 1912 with BELVEDERE	MISS L. SILCOX
1893	PUTNEY (originally EAST PUTNEY)	MISS S. M. HUCKWELL
1895	NEWCASTLE (CENTRAL)	MISS M. MOBERLY
1901	BIRKENHEAD	MISS B. E. ANDERSON

It is estimated that upwards of 135,000 girls have been educated at the schools since their foundation. The number at present in the schools is nearly 15,000.

Bath

MISS D. J. CHAPMAN, MA

Bath High School, the seventh school of the Trust, started its life in 1875 with sixty pupils in one of the tall regency houses in Portland Place, under the headship of Miss Susan Wood, who had been one of the early Girton students.

A search for knowledge has always ranked high among the school's aims. Because of the intellectual ability of women like Maria Grey and Mary Gurney, and their conviction that girls would enjoy studying at a serious level, full opportunities were given from the beginning for the study of mathematics, classical and modern languages, as well as English, history, and geography. Science was confined to botany, and domestic science and physical training were still in the future: games were not to come until fashion in dress allowed greater freedom of movement. There were no societies either, for before the coming of buses or trams, girls were not tempted to linger after school. But lack of out-of-school activities was not a drawback, for to the girls of this early period the excitement of work was the thing that mattered.

By the turn of the century the school had been in existence for twenty-five years and changes had already begun. Drill found its way on to the time-table, and hockey, cricket, and boating clubs flourished on a voluntary basis. Premises were enlarged, and the two houses on either side of the original, No. 5 Portland Place, were acquired. It is interesting too that Miss Shekleton, who was headmistress from 1898 to 1907, was the first woman to be co-opted on to the new Bath Education Committee.

The First World War brought no major change to the school, but in the years following great developments took place. By the mid twenties the houses in Portland Place had become too crowded, and in 1924, Rock House was bought from Miss Hope, a prominent figure in Bath society, and rechristened Hope House; in 1926 the new school was formally opened by the Marquess of Bath. The next ten years saw the school expand in every direction. In 1932 Beechen Cliff House was taken over from Ellen Linsley, herself an old girl, and in the same year the gymnasium was erected, while four years afterwards the Lansdown junior school was built. The numbers in the school were now 220 and all seemed set for a period of peaceful educational development.

It seems ironical that the Second World War should have brought disaster, for Bath was considered a safe area, and the school was filled with evacuated pupils from many of the Trust's London schools. But on the night of 24 April 1942, in the unexpected raids on Bath, the main building received a direct hit, other bombs falling in the grounds. The Trust, with courage and vision, immediately found temporary quarters in

Lansdown Crescent, and drew up plans for the reconstruction of the school as soon as government permits could be obtained, and much is owed to the drive and enterprise of Miss Blackburn, who, as a very young headmistress, accepted the challenge of organizing and building up the school at this difficult time.

It was in May 1951 that HRH the Duchess of Gloucester performed her first public act as Patron of the Trust schools by opening the reconstructed Hope House. It is indeed a lovely building: built in cream-coloured stone, it combines the graciousness of the old with the free uncluttered lines of the new. The fine Adam fireplace, the beautiful ironwork of the staircase, the intricate fingerplates of the doors in the hall, all salvaged from the old building, seem entirely at home in the lightness of a design adapted to the movements of the modern schoolgirl. And the view from the garden is superb as we look down upon the city of Bath with the hills beyond.

A thriving school is a living, growing community. Our numbers doubled and the school would not fit back into its original buildings. Our two boarding houses also are separated from each other physically, though administratively they are one unit, and our junior school expanded to overflowing, so that the top forms had to be housed in No. 12 in the Crescent. Our temporary quarters – the lovely Crescent houses – had to be retained, but as we run between buildings, their graciousness and the magnificent view do much to compensate for problems of organization and our hilly terrain.

Since our return to Hope House, our history has been one of further growth and adaptation. We have had welcome additions to our buildings. Two new laboratories were built in 1961 to meet the demand for advanced scientific studies, and in 1966 we acquired a beautiful library, which seats sixty with ease and has plenty of shelf space. Our garden is a delight – terraces, a rock garden, a rose garden created by our gardeners with loving care from amid the bomb damage; and surely few schools can boast a flourishing gentian and a judas tree.

Today the school has nearly six hundred pupils with over one hundred sixth-formers and there is constant pressure for places. Exciting developments have taken place in all subjects, involving new methods and new materials. Modern mathematics gives a better grasp of concepts; language teaching has changed fundamentally, activities in science lessons range from experiments with radioactive materials to the manufacture of cosmetics in sixth-form general chemistry lessons. Field courses are an integral part of the work in geography and biology, regular exchanges are undertaken with schools in France, Germany, and Greece, and studies are supplemented by welcome invitations to lectures at Bath and Bristol universities. Sound scholarship and a love of learning are all-important, but wide interests are also encouraged. Many girls learn to play stringed or wind instruments, the orchestra is flourishing, and we join in concerts, dramatic productions, and vigorous debates with neighbouring boys' schools.

A young woman of a century ago would certainly find life in the present

sixth form different, probably bewildering. Uniform was abandoned at this level many years ago and changing fashions have seen miniskirts, maxicoats, and trouser suits: in physical education girls may choose golf, judo, or trampolining instead of the more conventional teamgames and take part, if they wish, in holiday adventure courses and skiing trips abroad. There is a wide interest in world affairs (which befits young women who will be entitled to vote before they leave school) and our boarders from Malaysia or Iran and those whose parents are in Pakistan or the West Indies often help us to a better understanding of the problems. The girls are much concerned with social questions; corporate efforts are made for good causes and sixth-formers give practical help in their own time, visiting the elderly or helping with handicapped children.

In addition to all this there is an enormous wealth of career opportunities. It would surely rejoice the hearts of our founders to see our young women holding their own in the fields of medicine, law, computer science, archaeology, and estate management, and even winning places to study engineering at the men's colleges in Cambridge!

We need further buildings, of course, and as I write there are exciting and imaginative plans afoot which will enable us to concentrate our laboratories in one block, to bring the senior school on to the main campus and to provide more realistic accommodation for our sixth form. We combine planning for the future with pride in the past and recently have been pleased to take part in a scheme to restore the lamps to the lovely ironwork settings in the Crescent.

We, in Bath, are fortunate. We have such a goodly heritage in the aims and traditions of our school, we have the historic and literary heritage of our lovely city and the graciousness of our own buildings. We pay tribute to those who, during the last one hundred years, have shown such wisdom and foresight and have given so much. As we experiment and adapt to modern developments it is our responsibility to see that we too are building soundly for those who will follow during the Trust's second century.

IMMODESTY?

'An annual gym display was started for [an audience of] mothers only and fathers who were doctors.' (Tunbridge Wells 1901-11)

Birkenhead

MISS F. KELLETT, BA

Birkenhead High School was founded by a limited company in 1884 and became in 1901 the thirty-eighth and youngest Trust school. In 1905 its twenty-five girls moved into the present house at No. 86 Devonshire Place. Our main building reflects its origins. The gatepost displays the name 'Belgrano' cut deep into the stone. This is the name of a suburb of Buenos Aires to which the previous owner's fleet of tea clippers sailed out to found his fortunes. It must have been an imposing house, fit for the shipping magnates of those days. It is a tall building because, we are told, its owner liked to command a wide view as from the look-out of a ship. Within are steep and narrow staircases suggesting a ship's companion-way, and from some of the upper classrooms one may see far away beyond the roofs and treetops the cranes and funnels of Merseyside under a sky with those unmistakable cloud patterns which belong to the sea.

Since the house has belonged to us it has been gathering about it other buildings which a flourishing school requires. Junior school and sixth-form houses stand side by side in the grounds and the middle school house is across the road next to the local tennis club. There is shortly to be a foot-bridge across from senior school and then we shall no longer see members of staff dressed as lollipop men directing the traffic between lessons. A new classroom block was added in 1955, six new science laboratories complete with balance room, dark room, and preparation rooms in 1961, and a new dining room, kitchen, and hall in 1964. The previous hall is now used as a reference library and provides very pleasant working space for a hundred readers. The parents presented us with a beautiful new lecture theatre in 1971, and in 1974 the Trust is to build a new two-storey art centre adjacent to the hall.

Our peaceful surroundings are still enlivened by the sound of ships' sirens reminding us of our proximity to the river Mersey and the city of Liverpool, and we value our connections with the university and with our sister school, Belvedere, 'across the water'. Many parents are connected with the university and we are proud to have three Liverpool professors among our Local Governors. We have many connections, too, with some of the great industries of Merseyside – Cammell Laird, Lever Brothers, Lee's Tapestry Works, Bibby's, and Shell – and with Bidston Observatory where tide tables are compiled for Britain and most of the world.

Sir Wilfred Grenfell of Labrador in his speech at the prizegiving of 1927 urged the school to buy a playing field by its own exertions. This was done, and old girls tell of repeated sessions of stone collecting before the field could be used. We are fortunate, today, in inheriting this large field which is so conveniently close to the school.

Miss J. M. H. McCaig was headmistress at that time, and endeared herself to all with whom she came into contact by the force and sincerity of her character and her delightful personality. She left in 1930 to become headmistress of Notting Hill & Ealing.

Memorable occasions in the school's history are the distribution of prizes in September, 1908, by HRH Princess Louise and the visit of HRH the Duchess of Gloucester, to open the science wing and lay the foundation stone of the present assembly hall/dining room in our diamond jubilee year, 1961. These events took place during the headship of Miss P. Winter, the distinguished classicist who happily continues her association with the Trust by presiding over the inter-schools Greek and Latin prize competitions. We have also been happy to share the pride of Birkenhead in the launching of the Ark Royal by the Queen Mother from the ship-building yards of Cammell Laird and, more recently, in the opening of the second Mersey tunnel by HM the Queen.

Today we have dramatic, film, debating, and scientific societies and bridge, chess, and sailing clubs. Wartime entries in the Log Book show a different kind of activity. A telegram signed by the 'Officers and Crew of the Norwegian Minesweeper Polar VI' refers to the 'Trawler Committee' which made and collected comforts for the seamen, including knitted socks with pace eggs in the toes. On a more domestic note, our friendship with Shrewsbury High School goes back to 1939, when Shrewsbury generously received Birkenhead girls as evacuees. How fortunate the school was to have Miss Stephen as headmistress then to organize the evacuation, and how intimately, to this day, she remembers all her former pupils!

It is not minesweepers afar off but our own immediate environment in the nineteen seventies that claims the attention of Birkenhead girls in their leisure time. Many of them do useful service in the Wirral Associated Schools Project and the Young Volunteers of Merseyside, wielding litter collectors on the beach, helping the infirm in Cheshire Homes and looking after local children in play centres organized by the Probation Officer.

In 1971, the school's seventieth birthday year, there were 804 girls in school, including a junior school of 166 and a sixth form of 172. Of the 86 girls in last year's upper sixth no fewer than 55 are now reading for degrees in a wide variety of subjects at universities and polytechnics throughout the country. A further sixteen are studying to be teachers, three are on voluntary service abroad and the others have taken up courses and posts which are rewarding in themselves. Prospects for academic success next year are enhanced by the announcement of two scholarships to Oxford, two more entrances to Oxford, and three to Cambridge.

The classics staff have recently embarked upon the Cambridge Latin Course with its modern, oral approach to life in classical times. The Joint Matriculation Board has called upon us to do pre-tests in modern languages, Greek, and general studies and to try out experimental methods in German, Spanish, and English, thereby giving us an insight into the many stimulating changes taking place in methods of examining.

Girls attend courses in many subjects both at home and abroad and go on expeditions connected with almost every subject on the time-table.

Concerts and plays are annual events as they have always been – one of the first recorded school activities is of a dramatized performance of scenes from *Pride and Prejudice* given by the pupils of 1910. In 1971 we note the superb lead taken by an old girl, Patricia Routledge, in the new musical of *Pride and Prejudice* at the Birmingham Repertory Theatre. It was exciting, too, to hear another old girl, Janet Hughes, singing at Glyndebourne this year.

Lacrosse, tennis, and netball teams continue to distinguish themselves and the sixth-form physical education options include riding, squash, golf, judo, swimming, and sailing.

We try to move with the times. Our black and white uniform survives up to the fifth form but hats are optional. There is no prefect system. The School Captain, three Vice Captains, and four House Captains are elected to office and other responsible duties are carried out by volunteers. School lunch arrangements have a new look and self-service with considerable choice of menu has proved popular with all age groups.

In victorian days the main building owned a paddock and a pony, stables with hay in the loft, and a large and gracious garden. The gardens are still gay and well-tended, but ponies are only to be seen on the days of the Parents' Summer Fair, when buildings and grounds are transformed and parents succeed in raising in one afternoon the magnificent sum of £1,400 for the school.

Our links with the past are constantly strengthened at frequent gatherings of the Old Girls' Society in Birkenhead and London. Their most distinguished representative, Dame May Curwen, awarded the Nansen Medal for her work with refugees, visited us in 1972. We hope we proved to her that the youngest school of the Trust is a vigorous and lively community with a real sense of purpose and a sincere concern for people everywhere.

Blackheath

MISS M. ABRAHAM, MA

In 1878, in his drawing room, the Revd. E. Wilton South, headmaster of the Blackheath Proprietary School for Boys, met Mrs William Grey (Maria Grey), Miss Emily Shirreff, and about one hundred Blackheath residents. Their purpose was to discuss the possibility of a High School for Girls in Blackheath, and the result was an approach to the Council of the Girls' Public Day School Company. The necessary shares were taken up and when the search for a suitable house proved fruitless, an architect was called in and Blackheath became the first and only Trust school to open in purpose-built accommodation. The hall, interesting and unusual, has been described as a place of dignity, grace, and light; it continues to make a lasting impression, even on visitors who may see it only once. Considered spacious then, it remains a focal point, though we now have the best of both worlds, of the old and the new, since in 1967, the hall/gymnasium was completed, more functional, more obviously utilitarian, but equally light and attractive in its twentieth-century manner.

The school was opened in January 1880 by the Princess Louise with sixty-eight names on the register and with a curriculum seen by many contemporaries as dangerous: such education could only make the girls 'strong-minded', a dreadful fate indeed! Under the first headmistress, Miss Allen-Olney, life was 'impressively regular and orderly'; current ideas of discipline were rigid and the role of the pupils was passive – dictated notes copied neatly and then learned; modern languages taught in English and unintelligible when spoken. Yet within the first ten years, scholarships to Oxford, Cambridge, and Bedford College, London, had been won. In 1886 the appointment of Miss Florence Gadesden, an outstanding headmistress, set the seal on the school's reputation. A passionate educator, Miss Gadesden inspired staff and pupils alike with her own love of knowledge and freedom, and the reduction of school rules to a minimum soon gave rise to order based on understanding and self-discipline. Development was spectacular; the school's work was chosen for international exhibitions as far afield as Chicago and Allahabad, and ex-Blackheath pupils were in the vanguard of the 'Women's Lib' movement of their time, to secure recognition of women's intellectual ability. By 1926, twenty-one former members of staff, a number of them past pupils also, were headmistresses; two were principals of Technical Colleges, and Miss Major was Mistress of Girton.

But Miss Gadesden, and by implication Blackheath High School, took the lead in other directions. She startled contemporary opinion by allowing short skirts for gymnastics and games, a spectacle witnessed in 1912 by twenty-seven headmistresses, many of whom introduced the change into their own schools. She suggested the Lawn Tennis Union which grew into the Trust Tennis Rally; lacrosse was introduced in 1908; societies were organized and emphasis was placed on the duty of looking to the needs of others. At the same time, the tradition of self-help was established; in 1929, under Miss Gale, the objective was to drain the playing field and build the pavilion; in 1972 it is to modernize and extend the same pavilion.

Miss Gale had the difficult task of succeeding Miss Gadesden: she made her own contribution through her interest in individuals and the Old Girls' Association, and by her emphasis on the value of scholarly work. Miss Lewis, appointed in 1931, had to face the great upheaval of evacuating the school to Tunbridge Wells in 1939. She was headmistress of both schools by 1940, fused the best from each and retired in 1945 when the amalgamated schools returned to Blackheath.

In March of that year, the buildings had been badly damaged by a rocket, and Venus, whose plaster presence had graced the hall for so long, disappeared for ever. But under the steady and determined leadership of Miss Janet Macaulay and a band of workers, skilled and unskilled, the school was repaired and opened on time in September. A house in Morden Road was bought for the junior school; the numbers in the sixth forms grew steadily; and Miss Macaulay suggested that money raised during the celebrations of the school's seventy-fifth anniversary should provide the nucleus of a building fund for a hall/gymnasium.

Miss Macaulay's successor, Miss Wheatley, continued to campaign in the interests of getting the hall built and it was due to her unremitting efforts that the Parents' Building Fund Committee was set up and a covenant scheme introduced. The Committee gradually evolved a programme of fund-raising and social activities from which the school has benefited considerably over the years. When the hall/gymnasium was finally completed in 1966, at a cost of over £30,000, parents and staff, pupils past and present had shared in the raising of £12,000 towards that total. Nor were the benefits conferred by the new building limited to the vastly improved facilities available for physical education, for the production of plays and the performance of concerts. The site of the senior school is so circumscribed geographically that one can never start from scratch, but it was now possible to convert the old gymnasium into a library with custom-made furniture and later fitted with a carpet, in the interests of silence! The old library gave extra space for the provision of dinner, and the additional shelving in the new library made it possible to free a small room, previously used as a library extension, for sixth-form accommodation. Other changes, too, were made to extend the amenities and to keep in line with modern educational trends. The little-used domestic science room was converted into a geography room, and other rooms were adapted for subjects as far as was possible. Finally, the science accommodation, advanced for the times when it was built but inevitably outmoded by present-day standards, is being overhauled. Building a new art studio has made possible the conversion of the old art room into a modern biology laboratory and a preparation room. Plans for the complete reformation of the chemistry laboratory are on the board and we hope that similar improvements for physics will follow fast.

Nor has the junior school been forgotten. The nature of the grounds and buildings made it possible to plan for the construction of a separate infants' block, and the first instalment, the formroom for the kindergarten, was in use in 1963. This project was completed in 1971, when the second room, for the transition, was put up with incredible but most welcome speed in the summer holiday. The junior house has moved from strength to strength, first under Miss Booth and now with Mrs Masters. It combines in an imaginative way the conservative and the progressive, with a stimulating yet secure atmosphere made possible by a staff alert to the needs of the children and to the trends of education today. The wide-ranging interests of the staff, and the enterprising use of the lovely buildings and grounds, make the junior school an exciting place.

Today, nothing is sacrosanct: clear judgement is needed to see beyond fashionable ideas and practice to what is of fundamental worth in the way of progress, while preserving what is of proved and still relevant value from the past. The substitution of an 'At Home' under our own roof for a prize-giving in a distant town hall; the spreading of responsibility among all the sixth instead of a small prefectorial body; the introduction of general studies and Russian, of optional games and a wider range of physical activities at the top of the school; the opportunities for Holy Land cruises and visits to Russia, for pony-trekking and skiing, for helping with Task Force and enjoying American Field Scholarships; all these and a steady, relentless pursuit of sound learning and scholarship add up to an educational programme in the spirit, we believe, of the enlightened Miss Gadesden. We know that she would approve of the length of our gym skirts: we hope that we measure up also to the high standards she set in the exercise of freedom and self-discipline, in eagerness to learn and in acceptance of the need to develop one's talents to the full in order the better to serve others. Her generation did much to unseal the fountain: ours must ensure that our pupils learn to drink wisely.

STAFF TRENDS

'*In those days* (1917) *the staff was quite a small one and used to sit round the fire in the staff room after dinner and play guessing games.*'

'*We went to a factory to paint graduations on aeroplane parts. The first appearance of married members of staff was a surprise.*' (1914-18)

Brighton & Hove

MISS J. P. TURNER, BA

Brighton High School (Hove was not included in the title until 1912) was the tenth school founded by the Company and began on 13 June 1876, when seventeen pupils assembled at Milton Hall, Montpelier Road. The first headmistress was Miss Creak; some say she was under twenty-one when she was appointed, and that for the first month or two she was worried lest the papers she signed should not be legally valid as she was under age, and no one says she was more than twenty-three. Under her leadership the school rapidly grew in size, and in 1880 moved to 'The Temple'.

This curious and attractive building had originally been the country house which Thomas Kemp built for himself in 1819. It gained its name because it was supposed to have been made to the exact measurements of Solomon's Temple, and the pilasters on either side of the windows on the ground floor were made to represent inverted cannon, to commemorate the end of the Napoleonic Wars. For this reason, it was long known as the Temple of Peace. This is still the main building of the school, but the dome unfortunately had to be abolished to make room for larger science laboratories, and a new wing was added to the south side. Although the original wall of Thomas Kemp's garden remains, houses have sprung up all round the once isolated building which looked straight down to the sea. The next house to be built near was the old vicarage of Brighton, erected in 1834, and taken over by the school for junior pupils in 1922.

The curriculum of the school in the early years was surprisingly wide, as we learn from the report of the first prizegiving, which was held in 1884. 'Latin, Grammar, Mathematics, Chemistry, Geography, Art and Music', are all mentioned as gaining praise from outside examiners, and though the headmistress found it necessary to say that girls were sometimes kept away from school for frivolous reasons, such was the enthusiasm of the girls themselves that in the following year 'The Temple Club' was started, a weekly literary society for old girls. The list of books they read is impressive: 'In English, Motley's *Rise of the Dutch Republic* and Shakespeare's *As You Like It*; in Latin, Virgil's *Aeneid, Book viii*; in German, Schiller's *Maria Stuart.*' There is a note added that 'French Readings will be arranged as soon as possible'. The school library still has, as some of its treasured possessions, six volumes of his own works presented by John Ruskin, and the letters he wrote to the head girl when she invited him to come and address the school.

The idea that girls should do the same subjects as their brothers was rapidly gaining ground, but there were still doubts whether they could stand it physically; at the prizegiving of 1886 the Chairman urged parents

to see that children did their homework without interruptions – 'if that were done . . . there need be no apprehensions as to the education of girls involving, or almost involving, the extinction of the human race (applause)'. Could he have seen the school today, he would have realized such fears were groundless. From their early days, the girls displayed a love of games as well as academic studies. Hockey was not started until about 1895, but in 1884 there was most surprisingly a Football Club. There is an injunction in an early magazine not to 'hop over the ball instead of kicking it', but apparently the players soon grew much more expert and courageous. Parents complained that they wore out their shoes on the gravel, a window was broken, and, after the headmistress made the rule that the ball was never to be kicked unless on the ground, the enthusiasm for the game waned and the club was finally disbanded. Classes at a neighbouring gymnasium in 1889 resulted in a great improvement in deportment, and it was noticed that several of the girls had grown taller!

From the very beginning the girls were encouraged to take a practical interest in others less fortunate than themselves, and the present Guild for Social Service has had an unbroken career. Its activities have widened considerably since the early days when each member made at least one useful garment for the girls of the Servants' Home, and sometimes entertained the little servants to tea; but the spirit of the Guild is still the same, and the members give their help as well as their subscriptions, many girls paying regular weekly visits to elderly and lonely people, a friendship which often continues for some years.

The school has grown and grown; under each headmistress some acquisition has been made – Miss Creak moved to The Temple, Mrs Luxton added the new wing, Miss Lunn an extra storey and a new gymnasium in the grounds, Miss Lewis acquired the Old Vicarage for the Junior School and the present playing field, Miss Farquhar had the rough ground cleared and two better tennis courts made, and another boarding house was added in her day. To Miss Lockley the school owes the new part of the boarding house, new classrooms in the junior school, and the canteen in the grounds of the Old Vicarage; and during Miss Ashcroft's headship the cloakroom was extended, better provision was made for the secretarial staff, the new science building was opened, and the top floor of The Temple converted into a library and sixth-form rooms. Though the history of the present boarding house dates from 1912, from the earliest days the school had girls from outside Brighton who lived in a boarding house, run as a private venture but approved by the school authorities.

These, however, are all outward changes. School life today is perhaps more full than it used to be, but reading through the early magazines one is struck by the similarity rather than the difference, surely the greatest tribute to the far-sightedness and progressive policy of the founders and the early headmistresses. Pupils gave concerts as they do today, there were parties at the end of the term, and though a regular dramatic society was still in the future, in 1885 the girls were acting scenes from Shakespeare, and on an afternoon in July 1888, in a great burst of versatility, they presented scenes from *Alice in Wonderland* and *Through the Look-ing Glass*, a scene from *Henry VIII*, a Greek Tableau, and ended with a flower chorus – to say nothing of the songs, recitations, and piano solos which also found a place in the entertainment.

Buns and milk were sold at break as far back as the eighteen eighties, though there seems to have been more variety then. In the 'suggestions' page of the magazine for 1892 there is rather an appealing letter from a junior: 'Dear Editor, Allow me to suggest that we should have more than four sorts of penny buns, jam tarts with plenty of strawberry jam, is (sic) nicest.' Calorie-conscious girls of today prefer fruit and nuts.

Brighton & Hove has been an especially fortunate school in keeping an unbroken link with one of the founders of the Trust through the friend-ship of Lady Buxton, great-niece of Lady Stanley, whose yearly birthday parties at Newtimber Place became a tradition still most generously carried on by Mrs Clay, Lady Buxton's grand-daughter. Several girls in school today are the great grand-daughters of old girls and at least one family has been represented in all four generations.

Through all the years one is struck by the zest with which the staff and girls have combined to produce the best in both work and play, and in nothing is the continuity of their spirits more apparent than in the steady record of university successes and in the ever-growing variety of careers for which the pupils enter. As long ago as 1894, horticulture at Swanley is suggested as a suitable career. From the very earliest days Brighton & Hove girls won many academic successes, sending a steady stream of scholars to the universities of Oxford, Cambridge, and London. The school has progressed through many stages from an independent school run by a limited liability company to a direct grant grammar school of the same company, now formed into an educational trust, but there is no apparent difference. There has always been the same identity of interest and the same feeling of friendship between all branches of the com-munity, the same interest in learning, the same gaiety, the same joy in living.

Bromley

MISS P. M. F. REID, MA

'We have pleasure in drawing the attention of the Council to this town as a convenient centre for the establishment of one of their schools. The . . . want of a high-class school for girls is seriously felt. . . . If the Council should decide to open a School in Bromley, we have good reason to believe that it would be highly successful.' Thus ran the petition which was considered and later approved by the Council. A house was acquired in Elmfield Road, 'close to the London, Chatham and Dover Railway Station', at a rental of £134, on a twenty-one years' lease, with the right to purchase within three years for £2,500, and after alterations had been made at a cost of £175, Bromley High School opened on 18 January 1883, with twenty-three pupils, for the school 'did not meet with an enthusiastic welcome from Bromley folk'. Four years later that number had grown to 119, justification of the belief of the petitioners, and proof, perhaps, that the proximity of the railway station was a distinct advantage in those days, when as the first headmistress, Miss Heppel, remembers, 'Bromley was a small country town surrounded by pleasant woods and meadows. What is now Highland Road was a wood, where we gathered bluebells.'

Miss Heppel (1883–1908), and her successor, Miss Hodge (1908–24) both came to Bromley from Notting Hill, the second of the schools to be opened by the Council. They brought with them the high standard of scholarship that had characterized the founders of the Girls' Public Day School Company, and their own strong interest in languages. According to one of the first pupils, Miss Heppel was 'an expert' in French, and engrained in her pupils 'habits of accuracy by the scrupulous care she always gave to lessons in our early mathematics, as well as those in translation from any foreign tongue into our own'. Miss Heppel cared too about the school's games, charitable work, and social activities.

The school's charitable work began in 1888, in connection with the Waif & Stray Society, and in 1892 Bromley High School adopted its first orphan, Marian Holstein. The record of the school published to commemorate its golden jubilee in 1933 contains a number of references to such work. It was under Miss Heppel, too, that Bromley twice, in 1894 and 1901, played in the Tennis Shield Finals and, in 1900, in the Hockey Cup Finals. Miss Heppel was a keen horsewoman, and on occasions would ride up to London for a consultation at the Company's head office.

Under her successor, Miss Hodge, the school was further extended. Miss Hodge records that in 1908 there were 184 pupils, and that 'the building consisted of the original house, the large hall with the three classrooms underneath, and the three classrooms at the end of the passage, one on the ground floor and the other two up the staircase. The studio was in the gallery of the hall, a most inconvenient arrangement. . . . The hall had to be used for singing and all physical exercises, so it was no easy matter to draw up the time-table, as, of course, it had always to be free during recreation for use on wet days.' The school's many social activities were much curtailed by the war, and constant air raids meant a great strain on the girls, 'but they always turned up at school the next day, however long they had been kept up at night by the thunder of the guns'. After 1918, the school becoming rapidly larger in numbers and consequently over-crowded, Miss Hodge was quick to seize opportunities of enlargement, and The Hawthorns was bought in 1920 to provide a house for the junior school; and it was again Miss Hodge who initiated plans for a gymnasium, two new classrooms, and a studio on the top floor. These were opened in 1925, and must have been sorely needed, as by the time of Miss Hodge's retirement in July 1924 the numbers had risen to 400. It was in 1925, too, that the sports ground was acquired, again a very necessary addition, for by 1920 Bromley was playing both netball and cricket as well as tennis and hockey, and had by 1923 twice won the Junior Netball Cup and once shared the Senior Cup with Clapham.

In 1932 Miss Littlewood wrote for the school's jubilee publication that she was sure that during the next fifty years there would be 'holidays when no structural addition or alteration is made, when no rooms are changed or refurnished and we shall return to find the school as we left it at the close of the last term'. That was the period that saw the opening of the 'new wing', containing the library and classrooms; it also saw the re-organization of the curriculum. The standards then hoped for by Miss Littlewood are still, we trust, maintained, and we hope that we still deserve the commendation of the Inspector who wrote, after a full inspection in 1935: 'The school is a *good* place for girls to be in.'

As well as high standards of scholarship, which have ensured a steady stream of entrants to the universities (including around twenty places to read medicine in the last three years) and a number of distinguished old girls in many professions, the school has a tradition of music-making and musical achievement and of dramatic performance. The school orchestra was first formed in 1906, and there is a photograph hanging in Elmfield House showing an orchestral rehearsal in 1908; in 1913 Bromley High School 'shared with Sutton the honour of providing the orchestra under the able leadership of Miss Kimpton (whose name is commemorated in the Gwynne Kimpton Prize) at the banquet held at the Savoy Hotel . . . in connection with the Building Fund of the GPDS Trust.' The dramatic society dates back to 1921.

Apart from the air raid shelters still standing in the playground, there was a halt in the school's physical expansion from 1932 until after the Second World War, when Speldhurst was purchased in 1946, during Miss East's headship, and Oakdene in 1948. To Miss Leale we owe the opening in 1961 of the science laboratories and the acquisition of Elmfield House, which now houses all the music rooms and the upper sixth studies. And so the school has grown from 23 to around 700 during its eighty-nine years, and has seen seven headmistresses.

The school owes much to the spirit of the founders of the Girls' Public Day School Company and of its early headmistresses; they all shared a love of excellence and a love of people. Miss Littlewood tells us that Miss Hodge was 'outstandingly happy in all human relationships', and her successors continued to build on 'foundations of generosity, sacrifice and enthusiasm', undaunted by any realization of a 'generation gap' which existed in 1884 perhaps more clearly than now, since Mrs William Grey (Maria Grey) said then to the pupils of Bromley High School at their prizegiving: 'The young . . . seem to attach little value to the experience and wisdom of the old or past ages, and are apt to think that wisdom came into the world with their generation.' But each generation seems to grow to an appreciation of the past and to hope for the future.

I am fortunate to begin my term of office at a time at least as exciting as the early days of the school. 1972 sees the centenary of the GPDST itself; 1973 brings the school's ninetieth birthday. Perhaps it will be in 1974 that we shall, as we hope, move to new buildings on a spacious site of twenty-five acres in Blackbrook Lane, and then in 1983 will follow the school's own centenary. And so Miss Littlewood's 'next fifty years' will have seen a period in which 'no structural addition or alteration is made', but it will also have seen the long-looked-for move to new buildings, set in their own grounds, and away from the 'London, Chatham and Dover', now Bromley South Station, and once more near to woods – though I doubt that I shall ever ride on horseback to Queen Anne's Gate.

Croydon

MISS E. B. J. CAMERON, MA

In its beautiful building, on a sloping site of over twenty acres about three miles from the centre of the town, the inmates of Croydon High School enjoy the pleasure of trees and space. The pupils number about 1,120, almost 300 being in the junior school.

Like other Trust schools, it began in a small way. Under Miss Dorinda Neligan, eighty-eight pupils were on the roll when it opened in The Chestnuts, North End, Croydon in September 1874, but the numbers increased rapidly and some six years later 230 pupils moved to purpose-built premises at No. 36 Wellesley Road. The earliest time-table I have seen is that for 1875; teaching took place only in the mornings, four one-hour lessons being given daily, and between them was a short interval during which pupils were expected to walk round the corridor in an orderly manner. Talking was not allowed on the stairs. Far more preparation was set than is now. Almost every pupil had pianoforte lessons and was expected to do at least one hour's practice daily. Literature, composition, reading, history, geography, Latin, French, Euclid, arithmetic, and drawing were taught to the senior girls; drilling and 'tempest' were arranged on Wednesdays; I have been unable to find out what happened during 'tempest'! The instructor was for a time Sergeant-Major Burke, and drilling consisted of simple arm exercises and marching, but even this was not considered necessary after a while, though it could be taken by those who wished during 'recreation': the exercises consisted of picking up coloured ribbons from the floor without bending the knees, and marching round the lower cloakroom.

By the time the school was working in Wellesley Road, German could be studied as an alternative to Latin, scripture was taught as an afternoon lesson, and in 1885, hitherto almost unheard of for girls, chemistry was introduced, but of course at the beginning no practical work was allowed – it was dangerous! But the attitude to experimental science was changing, and in 1902, about a year after Miss Leahy succeeded Miss Neligan, a science demonstration room, forerunner of the laboratories, was built.

In the early days the girls did not wear uniform, and photographs show them decorously attired in the fashion of the time. By 1896 moderately short skirts were allowed for girls who attended Swedish drill classes in the Braithwaite Hall on Saturday mornings. Even in 1918 the gym mistress was requested to wear a long raincoat over her tunic when visiting other houses. For by this time the school buildings had been extended considerably by the successive acquisitions of three adjoining houses (occupied in part by the junior school and 'home life' training class) and of an outpost at Purley.

The school was growing enormously and as its golden jubilee approached Miss Leahy must have experienced a difficulty familiar to successors until the school moved to Selsdon: where were rooms to be found for the groups which had to be taught? A hall and adjoining classrooms were added – but a garden was lost. In Miss Neligan's careful handwriting we have a report for each year of her period of office. As early as 1884 she was concerned by the difficulties caused by public examinations, since the school was a Centre, and external candidates came to it. 'I feel sure that we shall be able for a long time to come to meet the wants of Croydon and its immediate neighbourhood in this respect. What I cannot do is to provide meals and sitting rooms both for candidates during the whole of the examination week . . .' she wrote in a letter to the Local Committee.

Miss Neligan had known other worries: letters 'from parents who never seem to read the prospectus' caused unnecessary correspondence, the kindergarten fees, at only two guineas a term, were less than those charged by private schools in the district and might make people imagine it less good than it was. Another anxiety was the presence of too many small boys in the preparatory department, which could hardly be said to act as a 'feeder' to the school.

During its first quarter century the school had moved from its original premises; during its second the new premises had been extended greatly and it had survived the First World War. The jubilee was celebrated in 1924 and with the third quarter century began a new era, under the headship of Miss Ella Ransford. This period covered the thirties, when there was high unemployment and financial difficulty in the country as a whole; it saw the rise of Hitler and Mussolini and again the clouds of war. Miss Ransford retired in 1939, having established the School Scholarship Trust to help with the continued education of girls, initially those who had left school. When Miss Adams arrived to take over the direction of the school, the Second World War had begun. She had just evacuated the Queen Mary High School from Liverpool and travelled to Croydon to find not 800 but 54 pupils, for many girls had been sent away to safe districts. Miss Adams had to act quickly to preserve the life of Croydon High School. Part of it was sent to Eastbourne, but as it turned out only for a while: the south coast, thought to be safe, was soon fortified and Llandilo then received part of the school, another group working in the outpost at Purley. The main cloakroom at Wellesley Road was strengthened, outside shelters were constructed and used by part of the school. But The Homestead became a YMCA hostel and The Elms a furniture store. Buzz bombs and V2s did their hateful damage and the school did not escape blast, but peace came at last. By the time the seventy-fifth birthday year came round numbers were large and the Parents' Committee helped to raise £500 for much-needed equipment. Miss Adams, knowing the school was firmly on its feet, set off on her first world tour.

Four years later the school celebrated its eightieth birthday and in a grand fête graciously attended by Her Royal Highness the Duchess of Gloucester, £950 was raised for the stage fund. But that was not enough. The school library was small and the accommodation for science inadequate. Miss Adams had been cherishing a dream and by 1959 it had become reality; the gymnasium was transformed into a magnificent library and thanks to the enthusiasm she engendered, gifts to furnish it and fill its shelves came pouring in. Meanwhile, industrial magnates of vision raised the Industrial Fund for the Advancement of Science to help to provide laboratory facilities for independent and direct grant schools. Croydon High School benefited, the physics and chemistry block, for which the Fund provided half the money, being opened by Sir Alexander Fleck, Chairman of ICI, on 10 March 1959, the day on which the Margaret Adams Library was opened by the Chairman of Governors, Lady Cash. So the old and the new were combined and when Miss Adams retired in 1960 her portrait, painted by Edward Halliday, was hung in the library which bore her name.

But in spite of the improvements in the school, the Council of the Trust was, as always, looking to the future. Croydon was changing fast, traffic was increasing and the growing school was being deafened by demolitions and throttled by office blocks. Not very long after I had become headmistress, Lady Cash asked me if I would welcome the prospect of a new building, if a suitable site could be found. This was exciting. A grey drizzle fell as the Duchess of Gloucester laid the foundation stone on 21 October 1964 and the Archbishop of Canterbury blessed it, and somehow, by September 1966, the school opened in unfinished buildings on its lovely site at Selsdon. The removal was a nightmare – and the first term too – but Mr Michael Greenwood designed a building which is now a pleasure to work in and to look at and in which, thanks to the magnificent work of the staff, of the late Mr E. H. Croston who was then the Trust surveyor, and the older girls, teething troubles were overcome and the school settled remarkably quickly. By 1967 we were ready for another royal visit and on a glorious May day the Duchess of Gloucester paid us the great honour of again coming to Selsdon, this time to see the school and declare it open. Every one was impressed by her graciousness and charm.

To be given such a splendid new school with excellent facilities both indoors and out at such a troubled period in educational history was an act of faith on the part of the Council. Now the parents have come forward and with the help of their daughters and Old Croydonians are raising money for the one facility we lack – a swimming bath. If, from the school, gracious, socially aware people emerge to continue with zest, but humility, the education they have received we hope that those who had faith in us will feel it was justified. Present Croydonians have inherited a fine tradition: unblemished and enhanced may future generations receive it from them.

Ipswich

MISS P. M. HAYWORTH, BSC

Forty-three girls met their new headmistress, Miss Sophie Youngman, on the morning of 30 April 1878 at the opening of the Ipswich High School in the Assembly Rooms in Northgate Street. The years between our foundation and the present time have been ones of such rapid change that probably none of those first pupils would recognize the High School of today as 'their' school – but, equally, few of the present girls spare more than a passing glance for Sketchley Cleaners in Northgate Street, now occupying the site of the original school, or look up to the façade above the shop front which is substantially unchanged since those days. Inside the school, classes had to be held in two large rooms, divided by curtains into six classrooms, and, perhaps because of this, a silence rule was strictly enforced except at breaks. At recreation, girls could buy a glass of milk and some biscuits – not so very different from the tuckshop of today – and groups were allowed out in rotation to take the air in the small concrete playground and to play on the 'giant stride'. Much in favour in late victorian days and well into this century, the 'giant stride' resembled a maypole, but with iron and chains replacing wood and ribbons, and could be rotated at speed whilst the expert users clung to the steel chains and swung themselves high in the air – or were dashed to the ground, with sometimes alarming results.

But there was relatively little play. The late Mrs Ethel Palmer (née Stevenson), a pupil from 1884 to 1887, recalled memories of that early school in the jubilee year of 1928. She wrote:

'It is more than forty years ago, at a time when a High School girl was considered to be the most modern thing alive, that I . . . a very shy girl of fourteen walked for the first time down from the hostel at Thorn Bank (then kept by Miss Sanderson and Miss Bidwell) to the tall old house in Northgate Street, and was swept into the hum and bustle of the school reassembling for the autumn term. Upstairs in the big room packed with girls, punctually as the clock struck nine, a small, slim, wiry lady came in, very dignified, . . . whose rare smile or slightest expression of approval were to mean so much to me during the next three years.

There was a hush while she read prayers, a first morning never to be forgotten. Then the different forms dispersed in order to their classrooms and work began.

A modern girl, who takes good teaching for granted; can have no idea of the revelation it was to a girl, accustomed to puzzle things out for herself, to be really taught Latin or mathematics, with illustrations and explanations on a blackboard. My home governess had given me an arithmetic book and said: "Read the chapter on decimals and work out the examples as well as you can." You can imagine the result!

We were extraordinarily happy. . . .'

Shortly after the school's fiftieth birthday Mrs Palmer endowed the scripture prizes which bear her name. Over the years other prizes have been given in memory of former governors, headmistresses, or members of staff. Perhaps the most notable endowment is that of the Clayden Travelling Scholarship, founded under the bequest of Miss Emily Ann Clayden in 1926 to enable past pupils of Ipswich High School to live abroad for a while in order to pursue a particular field of study, or post-graduate research. Awarded every five years, it is particularly appropriate that the scholarship is to be given again in 1972, the Trust's centenary year.

The foundation of a High School for girls was a daring venture, regarded with some misgiving in the town. Ipswich School had for more than three centuries seemed a right and proper place for a gentleman to send his sons – but what of his daughters? Miss Youngman's personality, tact, and wisdom ensured the success of the school and quickly won the support of well-respected local people, among them Lord John Hervey, Dr W. A. Elliston, Mr J. R. Jefferies, Mr R. L. Everett, Mr Henry Packard, and Mr B. B. Hunter Rodwell. In 1899 the Princess Louise visited the school to celebrate its coming of age and to honour the work of Miss Youngman, shortly to retire.

The school buildings in Northgate Street had twice been enlarged but continued growth made it necessary to search for more extensive premises and the *School News* of 1904–5 reported:

'The Council have purchased Brakefield (the residence of the late Mr Walton Turner) on behalf of the Ipswich High School. The school will remove to Brakefield immediately on the completion of the necessary additions and adaptations to High School requirements. . . . A laboratory is needed for the extension of science teaching, and the important part which outdoor games play in the school curriculum have induced the Council to look out for a site where a large playground, tennis courts, and hockey field could be attached to commodious school build-ings. This combination they believe they have secured in Brakefield. . . . The High School anticipates a future of increased happiness and usefulness.'

The extension to No. 26 Westerfield Road completed, the school moved in 1907 to its present home, or at least part of it. The site was indeed well chosen, in a road which even today is comparatively quiet and opposite to Christchurch Park with its lakes, its trees, and broad stretches of grass. Now, with the school swollen to over 570 pupils, our buildings sometimes seem far from commodious, but we still rejoice in our green vistas and our trees and suffer the attendant problem of vast accumulations of fallen leaves each autumn.

Woodview, the house adjoining Brakefield and now the sixth-form house, was secured for the school following a public appeal for funds in

1913 and early in 1920 the Council acquired the two houses in Westerfield Road next to Woodview. Of these, Wildersleigh (No. 32) was opened in September as a junior boarding house and Fernleigh (No. 30) was adapted as a junior school house, as it has remained ever since.

Thus by 1921 the greater part of the school buildings we know today were in use, although this use has in some cases changed with the years. The need now was for an improved games field, but it was not until 1954, whilst Miss Neal was headmistress, that the present field in Westerfield Road was bought, providing us with three hockey pitches, twelve tennis courts, and a wide view of rural Suffolk for the spectators.

Meanwhile, the buildings which had seemed so spacious in 1921 were again proving inadequate, and in 1935 the wing at the east end of the hall – the present gymnasium and physics laboratory – was added. The geography room, on part of the original flat roof of the gym, came much later in 1955. Until the 'new' science block of chemistry and biology laboratories was completed in 1960 the physics laboratory had perforce to serve also for biological work and chemistry was taught in the present pottery and craft room.

Miss Neal guided the school through some of the most difficult years of its history during the Second World War. For one term the Ursuline Convent High School from Ilford shared our buildings: Ipswich had lessons in the morning and Ilford in the afternoon and each school used unwanted corners in its off-session. Later in the war some girls were evacuated and the Army moved into part of our buildings. Numbers of girls and staff were sadly depleted, but the school weathered the storm and a period of growth and development followed the war years. Miss Neal retired in 1960 after a longer term of office even than Miss Youngman's, and one no less significant in fostering the standards and values we prize today. We are delighted to welcome Miss Neal to our carol service in December, and we are daily reminded of her in the selection of shrubs she chose for our front gardens, providing beauty in leaf or flower or berry at all seasons of the year.

The last decade has seen changes which themselves symbolize the marriage of old and new which has been characteristic of the school throughout its history: the opening of the science laboratories and, more recently, thanks to the generosity of many parents and friends, the new classroom block, their clear lines contrasting sharply with the victorian and edwardian buildings a stone's throw away; the acquisition and adaptation of Nos. 16 and 18 Westerfield Road to become the home of our preparatory department (unlike most of our sister schools we welcome boys as well as girls to our most junior forms); and the Fison Library, its striking modern design much admired by all visitors.

A centenary is a time both for looking back over the past ninety-four years and for looking forward: for looking back in gratitude to all those too numerous to mention by name – governors, members of staff, girls, and friends who have made the school what it is today – and for looking forward with confidence to our future. On Wednesday, 11 April 1899 the

East Anglian Daily Times, reporting the resignation of Miss Youngman, concluded its notice:

'. . . the schools, of which the Ipswich High School is one, have done wonders for girls' education in England. They have raised the standard of women's education to a point which compares not unfavourably with that of men, and have shown that this high culture is not inconsistent with other qualities in which women should chiefly desire to excel. The Ipswich High School can take its place among similar institutions in England without fear of comparison.'

May this be true for many centenaries to come.

Kensington

MRS J. BAYLDON

The oldest school of the Trust has become the 'baby' of that family, for Kensington, born in 1873, closed its senior school in 1948 and has since functioned as an independent junior school. The name 'Kensington High School' was preserved in the hope that at some time in the future a senior department might be reformed, and it was felt that the name of the very first school of the Girls' Public Day School Trust should not be allowed to die. The smallest school now, it has some 200 pupils whose ages range from five to twelve and a half years.

Opened on St. Agnes's Day, 21 January 1873, at Durham House, Chelsea, it was first known as the Chelsea School. Six years later it moved to Cromwell Road and in 1888 to St Albans Road, Kensington, where it became known as Kensington High School for Girls. In charge of both the moves was Miss Hitchcock, who remained headmistress from 1879 to 1900. Under her direction the school grew and prospered. The premises, which were to house the school until 1941, were written of with pride in the Kensington *Chronicle* of 1896: 'The lofty rooms, wide corridors, studio, sixth form room with its pleasant outlook on verandah and tennis court, and the assembly hall' – used for the Annual Conference of the Head Mistresses' Association that year.

In 1900 Miss Ethel Home was appointed headmistress, and during her thirty-one years at Kensington the school became famed for the excellence of its music teaching. A Music Training Department was established and many tributes were paid to Miss Home's brilliance as a lecturer in music. Amongst the pitifully few remaining records – all too many were lost when the building was destroyed in 1941 – there is a letter from Sir Robert Mayer to Miss Home praising the school's music, and her direction of it. Miss Home lived to attend the school's eightieth birthday celebrations in 1953.

In 1931 Miss Lilian Charlesworth became headmistress, bringing to the school all the qualities which made her one of the outstanding personalities in education. So much could be told of her success at Kensington, but it is the informal photographs of her at picnics with the prefects, her comments in the prefects' journal in her bold writing, which reveal the warmth of her personality and charm which endeared her to the girls.

In 1939 Miss Charlesworth was transferred to Sutton High School, Miss Marguerite Burke became headmistress and the school spent the autumn term at Oxford. Apart from this brief period the school continued to function in London throughout the war, largely through the vigour, determination, and persuasive personality of Miss Burke. When a landmine destroyed the school buildings in the spring of 1941, within a week Miss

Burke 'persuaded' the owner of No. 17 Upper Phillimore Gardens to allow the school to open there. Many exciting years followed. Carrying on the school under very difficult conditions, those who were privileged to work with Miss Burke began to feel that Kensington High School was indestructible.

In 1948, however, the building being inadequate for the growing numbers in the senior school and planning permission to build on the old site being refused, the Council decided with reluctance that the senior school must close.

The junior school, which had been housed in No. 5, settled happily into No. 17, where the girls were delighted to have so much space and a garden of their own. Miss Burke started this new venture, planning the curriculum, classrooms, catering arrangements, and uniform. The years which followed, with Miss Baker as headmistress, from 1948 to 1966, brought a high standard of achievement; many of the traditions of the old school were retained, and the music continued to flourish. One of the highlights of these years was the school's ninetieth birthday celebrations. On an icy day, 2 February 1963, after a service in St Matthew's Church, Bayswater, a party was held in the Kensington public library new hall. The climax came when Sir William Cash and the youngest and smallest child in the kindergarten cut the first slice from a yard square cake, decorated with the school colours and ninety candles.

Today, No. 17 Upper Phillimore Gardens is overflowing. Throughout the years since 1948 the school has steadily gained a reputation for high academic achievement. For every one child gaining a place in the school, the parents of at least four others have to be told that there is no place available. Ironically there is now not only a shortage of junior schools in Kensington but of senior school places as well. The fervent wish of all parents whose children attend the school is that they should continue there. Instead, places have to be found for them in other schools. Unhappily, travelling difficulties prevent many from staying within the Trust. Although each year one or two go on to Putney, Wimbledon, Notting Hill & Ealing, and South Hampstead, in the main St Paul's, Godolphin & Latymer and such boarding schools as Wycombe Abbey and Benenden are the schools to which the girls transfer. This year the senior, middle school, and under-twelve scholarships awarded at Wycombe Abbey are all held by girls from Kensington High School.

There is something akin to magic about No. 17 Upper Phillimore Gardens – when you have crossed the threshold and stand in the entrance hall with its bright red domed ceiling, it does not take long to realize that any child spending her early, formative years there is a very lucky little girl. Is it the house with its gracious rooms and lovely garden that brings the feeling of happiness? Or is it just because it is peopled by the very young? The young attack everything with such vigour, such abounding energy and enthusiasm. As they wear their coloured bows of ribbon, representing the various 'houses' in their music competitions and gym contests, they do not fully realize that they are carrying on the traditions started by their older sisters, almost a century ago.

There have of course been recent innovations; the yearly carol service at St Mary Abbot's Church, the highlight of which is always the carols composed by the girls themselves; the Summer Carnival when parents, old girls, staff, and girls turn the house and garden into a fairground for charity. The recent leavers return each year for a Christmas party and the upper thirds spend a week of the summer term at a Field Centre.

What of the future? There is a desperate need for a second house, but property in Upper Phillimore Gardens is not easy to obtain and is very expensive. It is fun to 'pot' in the pantry and paint in the dining room and to have a music lesson on the piano in the cloakroom. It is possible to set up experiments in the formrooms and to do dressmaking in the kindergarten – when the kindergarten is not there; all this is perhaps part of the charm of Kensington. But so much could be done with a little more space, space for a studio, a larger staffroom, more formrooms. Maybe our centenary year will be a lucky year and the right house will become vacant. In the meantime Miss Farrer at No. 1 plays fairy godmother and a beautiful room with grand piano is available at all times. It is used in the main for drama and music.

Plans are already under way for the centenary of the first Trust School, which falls on a Sunday, 21 January 1973. The plans are for a service in St Mary Abbot's Church and then a concert, in which old girls will join with present pupils to show that Kensington's music is still very much alive.

Although the senior school died in 1948 its spirit lives on in a small but loyal group of old girls of the senior school who meet in the school each year. It is a privilege to play hostess to them, and to listen to their hilarious stories of the war years at Kensington. Their affection for the school is something to treasure. Several have daughters at Kensington and from one of these came this term a tribute to the school. Just twelve years old, having spent a year very happily at her senior school she wrote, 'I suppose you will be busy testing the new "Kindies". How I wish I could be four again and then I would be looking forward to starting at Kensington High in September and to the six happiest years of my life.'

To the Council of the Trust the oldest, yet the youngest of the Trust say 'thank you' for creating us, preserving us, and supporting us throughout a hundred happy years.

THEN AND NOW—PHYSICAL TRAINING

Shrewsbury

Kensington

Liverpool: the Belvedere School

MISS M. C. L. WARD, BA

Founded like all other Trust schools in response to a request from local citizens, the Liverpool High School came into existence in 1880. Throughout its ninety years it has been housed at No. 17 Belvidere Road, an imposing villa backing on to Princes Park. Adjoining houses have been added from time to time, and one is now the junior school; in 1964 there was built between this house and the Park a modern block comprising twelve classrooms on three floors linked by a long corridor to Belvidere Road. Although we enjoy the amenities of the new building, we cherish our affection for the older houses and are particularly proud of our school hall, the music room of the original house, in spite of its inadequacy for its present purpose.

It was Miss Rhys (1903–22) who brought about the change in the school's name, partly because there were so many 'High Schools' in the district, partly because 'Belvedere' was richer in potential rhymes (all the school songs were written after the change). She was well pleased with the effects: 'It was Archdeacon Howson's address on "Belvedere and the Vision Beautiful" that helped us all to cherish the name as we do now. Every year, of course, adds to the wealth of happy associations with it, and I think the change has been a distinct gain.' Unfortunately, Miss Rhys did not succeed in changing the spelling of Belvidere Road.

The school very early developed its own characteristics and in many ways appears ahead of its times. Here is Miss Huckwell, second headmistress of Belvedere, speaking of the young school to which she came in 1883. 'The work was uphill, there were prejudices to be overcome, traditions to be established and the value of education and scholarship for girls to be proved and maintained. Then too the girls were not accustomed to accept voluntarily law and order, especially from a new-comer. . . . Self-determination in schools is no new thing, it was very vigorous and of an unruly type in the girls of 1883 in the Liverpool High School.' But if she was critical, she was also appreciative: 'In our girls we had very good material, high-spirited, intelligent and responsive. The relationship between them and their teachers was of the friendliest.' This is not unlike the school of today. Twenty years later Miss Rhys gives a slightly different picture: 'The school struck me as very quiet. There was supposed to be strict silence all day long except at play time and in the dinner hour. I changed this and allowed speaking in the cloakrooms and between lessons and then we began having prefects and monitors to see that the new freedom was used rightly.'

What a warning one old girl gives of the days before Belvedere had uniform: 'Our great joy', says she, 'was our promotion to the upper school cloakroom with its possibilities of trying on the prefects' hats. It was before school uniform was worn and some of the prefects used to wear marvellous hats trimmed with roses.' And again: 'When the badge on the blazer pocket was changed, many stormy meetings were held on the subject in the sixth-form room and it was some time before people would relinquish their individual tastes for scarlet or green and agree to keep the school blue with the school motto and monogram on the pocket in place of Minerva.' It is all so familiar, much like the School Committee's discussions in recent months.

It was Miss Rhys perhaps most of all who built up the school, strengthening its best traditions, setting the standards for the future, and establishing in the city of Liverpool its own place for the school. Her successors carried on her work, and are remembered by many old girls and former members of staff with affection and respect. Miss Cossey for example, although she came to Liverpool for only three years, having retired from Portsmouth, made an indelible impression, introducing the house system and the observance of the school birthday. Miss Cossey gave great pleasure by being present at the opening of the new building in 1964 and although she ended the day in hospital she characteristically declared she would not have missed the function for anything. All through her time in hospital she took a tremendous interest in what was going on in school and kept this up after she was allowed to return to Wales. A suitable memorial to her, a lectern, a table, and chairs for the hall platform, was acquired with a legacy she left us. Then there are many who still remember Mrs Hobson and her remarkable courage and tenacity in facing the difficulties of evacuation and the problems of building up the school after the war.

The school was always known for its high standard of academic work and sent up a steady stream of girls to the universities, but at no time was a narrow curriculum followed. Art had its place especially in the days of Miss Laverock, when the art students contributed a succession of hangings to the Walker Art Gallery.

From the beginning drama was a feature of the curriculum. In 1889 the *Antigone* was produced, and of this an old girl later wrote: 'The Council had never allowed us to dress up, so the parts of Shylock, King Lear, Wolsey were acted without the trappings that are such a help. Greek dress was considered seemly, so for the first time we felt the thrill of costume and simple scenery.' Surely it is not without significance that Belvedere was the first Trust school in which staff plays were produced.

In recent years the school has developed its music under the encouragement of parents famous in the musical world. The orchestra has been revived and musical instruments provided by the generosity of the Parents' Association. Girls have gone on both to study music at university and to become practising professional musicians. The orchestra and choir give great pleasure to themselves and to their audience. Their most recent achievement was an unforgettable rendering of Haydn's *Creation*, in which the school choir was augmented for the first time by fathers, brothers, and friends to provide male voices.

Physical education has not been neglected in spite of the dimensions of the gymnasium, regarded long since as 'antique', and the innumerable problems connected with the playing field. The school has maintained a high standard of lacrosse: more than once in recent years it has won the Cup for its section in the London tournament and twice running has been awarded the Holt Cup for the school which has most old girls playing in national teams.

The school has always shown a deep sense of responsibility to the community. Margaret Beavan, whose active concern for her fellow citizens led to her becoming the first woman Lord Mayor of Liverpool, was but one of those involved in social service. The tradition has been maintained and the Guild of Service, well supported by the upper part of the school, is of help to young and old, in institutions or at home. An Old Girls' Helping Fund, begun during the early days of the First World War to provide comforts for the troops, was maintained to help pupils in need and is still used for this purpose. For more than fifty years Miss Ella Read, one of the earliest women horticulturists, acted as treasurer.

When in 1964 we were the first girls' school in Liverpool to be recognized for the teaching of radioactive physics, we were only following our tradition. For science was taught long before it was customary in girls' schools. An old girl gives this account; 'The only laboratory of any sort was a small top room, with a gas jet and a tap in one corner of the room. . . . By the time I was old enough to be trusted with a test tube and a bit of magnesium ribbon the new laboratory over the gymnasium had been built. . . . Still further developments took place, the most important of which were the yet newer laboratories, on a far more extensive scale and well-equipped with apparatus, and yet again a little later in 1919 Room 7 was turned into an "A" Physics Laboratory – it was meant to be a temporary arrangement.' These are the same laboratories which are now in the process of being brought up to date.

But in spite of our lack of facilities we were on the right lines even in 1891, for in the *Chronicle* of that year we read of an appeal to the parents: 'The possession of specimens to illustrate natural history and other science lessons would be of the greatest value to us. Children learn so much through the eye, and by seeing a specimen they realise far more than any description of it would enable them to do.' This was the argument we put to the Parents' Association when we asked them to bear the cost of constructing the 'Mouse House', and they agreed. In fact there have always been good relations between school and parents. Miss Rhys said: 'It is one of the proud boasts of our school that we have educated the children of such a large number of distinguished citizens of Liverpool. I do not think there is any school in England where parents are such a tremendous help and whom it is always a pleasure to meet.' Every one of her successors would endorse her verdict.

Nor is pupil participation anything new. Among our archives is a printed report of a Conference on Education in 1917: not as you might suppose a conference of headmistresses, or perhaps of staff, but in fact a conference of the Belvedere headmistress, staff, and girls, the whole school discussing what should be taught and why.

As we look back at this time of the Trust's centenary we also look forward. Miss Rhys speaking at her last prizegiving said: 'The hall is one of the most beautiful school halls in England but is far too small for us now. I hope to be present at the opening of a big hall and gymnasium before many years pass.' That was fifty years ago; it is still our dream, and we look forward to its fulfilment within the next three years.

Belvedere has the reputation of being a happy school. Why? Surely part of the answer was given by an inspired child who wrote in a general knowledge paper at the time when the Girls' Public Day School Company became a Trust: 'A Trust School is one where the girls are trusted.' Or as her headmistress put it: 'One important thing in a school is that everyone should regard every single child as an individual and get every single girl to think that she counts and that she has got to do the very utmost possible with her life. That is what we try to do at Belvedere.' And she continues in words that contain a message for us today as we look forward to the future: 'We need not fear that anything will go wrong if we remember that a school is a place where growing goes on.'

EARLY IMPRESSIONS

'*If I had been asked what was my first pleasant impression of my school (and all my impressions were pleasant) I should have answered then as I do now, "that of law and order". I still remember with acuteness the joy with which I went home on my first real school day and told my mother I had a number!*'

'*Moving about the school was made very orderly by the rule which caused all girls to hold their left hands behind their backs when leading into the assembly room for prayers. As they held their books in their right hands they had therefore no free hand with which to pull another girl's hair or fidget.*'

Newcastle (Central)

MISS C. RUSSELL, BA

In September 1876 Gateshead High School opened at Prospect Cottage, Gateshead. Miss Rowdon was headmistress and she had twenty-eight pupils. The schoolroom was originally divided by a thick curtain, which could be drawn back for prayers and other occasions. The school was founded at the request of local families, who had a strong desire to provide a sound education for their daughters as well as for their sons. The people who were connected with the school in the early days had great foresight and determination and their imagination was fired with a vision of the possibilities which might open for girls if they could receive an education comparable in standing to that enjoyed by their brothers. So successful were they that, only nine years after its foundation, the school was in a fine new building with 300 pupils on the roll. The building had a science laboratory, which must have been a rather unusual feature in a girls' school at that time.

Miss Cooper, who was headmistress from 1879 to 1891, was long remembered with affection and admiration for the wonderful school she created. She collected round her an able, devoted staff who gave their fortunate pupils a stimulus which must have been rare at this period. Mr Leblique and his son, who taught gymnastics and fencing, are still remembered in the award of the annual prize which bears their name.

In 1889 a preparatory school, intended at first as a junior school for Gateshead, was opened in Newcastle; in 1895 it became a full high school with Miss Moberly, who had succeeded Miss Cooper at Gateshead, as its headmistress. Gateshead continued, under Miss Vickers and Miss Tooke, until 1907, when it was closed because of changing social conditions in Gateshead. Its remaining pupils were transferred to Newcastle.

The curriculum was designed to give a broad, liberal education. The early headmistresses believed passionately in the importance of the influence in society of the educated wife and mother and their great aim was to secure the recognition of girls' schools as an integral part of the national provision.

Memories and reminiscences of Miss Hiley, who was headmistress from 1911 to 1935, are still affectionate and vivid. She was one of the outstanding headmistresses of her time and we still benefit from the influence she exerted on the character of the school as a whole and on individual members of it. She died in December 1971 at the age of ninety-three; until about a year previously she kept in close contact with the school and followed its activities and achievements with eager, lively interest. She had a most modern approach to all aspects of contemporary education and her ready wit, her humour and calm wisdom, made both conversation and correspondence with her a great joy.

Miss Hiley guided the school through twenty-four difficult years which included the First World War and the great depression of the twenties. School numbers fluctuated from 145 when she came, to 450 immediately after the war, and later settled at about 330. The school uniform was changed from green to brown: the junior school moved, first to No. 3 Eslington Terrace and then to Jesmond Road; over £2,000 was raised to buy a playing field, and the beautiful library, a gift of Newcastle old girls, was sufficient for the school's needs until the great increase in sixth-form numbers which began in the late fifties.

Miss Odell succeeded Miss Hiley and had the onerous task of organizing the school's evacuation to Keswick in 1939. Miss Odell and Miss Leale, who succeeded her in 1940, overcame, with great resourcefulness, energy and cheerfulness, the many difficulties which faced them; the pupils who were evacuated, numbers of whom are parents of present pupils of the school, remember the period as a very pleasurable and somewhat adventurous experience.

In 1942 the school took over St Margaret's School, Gosforth, and some pupils went there, while others remained in Keswick. In January 1943 the whole school returned to Newcastle, the seniors to Eskdale Terrace and the juniors to Gosforth. Under Miss Leale's guidance, the school increased steadily in size and the sixth form, too, became bigger and more important. Gradually, more subjects were added to the curriculum, more importance was given to the teaching of sciences, the width of the school's interests was further extended by foreign contacts and great was the awareness of the increasing importance and value of the role women were being called upon to play in modern society.

The school was lively and happy when Miss Belton succeeded Miss Leale in 1949. Her standards were high and her interests wide. She encouraged initiative and a sense of responsibility in the girls and had the great gift of inspiring them all to do their very best in all spheres. The standard of the school's academic work was very high and a fairly even balance between arts and the sciences was achieved. Scope for initiative and responsibility was given by the various societies, which still flourish today. New ones are being established and the organizers continue to show skill and resourcefulness in the imaginative programmes of activities they arrange.

During the thirteen years which Miss Belton spent at the school, there were many new, exciting developments. A magnificent four-storey block, containing four large laboratories, a large studio, a comfortable, attractive staffroom, and a pleasant, modern library extension was built. The resulting loss of playing space was offset, to some extent, by the acquisition of Eslington Court. Physical work now included judo, fencing, archery, squash, riding, with pony-trekking, canoeing, and skiing holidays.

It is now nearly ninety-six years since Miss Rowdon assembled her first pupils at Prospect Cottage, Gateshead; throughout that time, many generations of pupils have benefited from the devoted service of people who have made invaluable contributions to the life of the schools in many ways. If one mentions names, it is because one thinks of them as representatives of so many others. Miss Linfield, who retired in 1956 after thirty-seven years in the school; Miss Forrest (1931-62), whose lessons in English literature are remembered with gratitude by many generations of sixth forms; Miss Crisp, who was head of the junior school for thirty years; and, more recently, Mrs Wilthew (1944-71), head of the mathematics department and careers mistress, and Mrs Greener (1944-70), head of sciences; Miss Petrie, a former pupil, who joined the junior school staff in 1945 and is still with us.

The school is greatly indebted, too, to its Local Governors and to their Chairmen. Professor Tuck, the present Chairman, has been a tower of strength throughout the difficult period of reorganization and the school has benefited greatly from his expert knowledge and his wise counsel. In their different sphere, too, Mr and Mrs Gibson should be mentioned for the full and active part they played in school life when they were caretakers for thirty-six years.

The Old Girls' Guild continues to be active and shows keen interest in the welfare of the present pupils. The traditions of the Guild go back to the Gateshead days when former pupils worked hard to raise money for such items as library furniture and musical instruments. Until 1962, former Gateshead pupils met annually for tea at school but this delightful custom had to be abandoned when numbers diminished and others were unable to travel. The present generations of pupils greatly value the strong links retained with their past through the Old Girls' Guild and are proud of the traditions which have been passed down to them.

The school of today retains its gaiety and sense of purpose and continues to play an active, useful part in the life of the community. Many girls are active in the Duke of Edinburgh's award scheme and others are well known to the sick and elderly and to the very young in the city through membership of such groups as the Young Volunteers. The curriculum continues to be widened to meet the needs of the modern age. There is still a solid background of scholarship as increasing numbers of girls embark on degree courses on leaving school each year. There are now 138 girls in the sixth form and they very much enjoy the freedom with responsibility which our acquisition of Eslington Tower as a sixth-form unit has brought to them. In spite of the efforts of the Playing Field Committee, the school has been unable to acquire a field of its own, but we have found a spacious field to rent on the Town Moor and another one is now amicably shared with the Church High School.

In 1971 a committee of parents, Guild members, governors, and staff formulated the idea of starting a Central Newcastle High School Association with a view to stimulating social activity and a general interest in education among its members and to provide a vehicle by which they could give collective help to the school. Much interest has been shown and we hope that it will be a great source of strength and support to the school in the years ahead.

Norwich

MISS D. F. BARTHOLOMEW, BA

It is a matter of great pride to us at Norwich High School that we were the first school of the Trust to be founded outside London. But this is not surprising. The famous families of Norfolk and Norwich, the Gurneys, the Barclays, the Buxtons, the Martineaus, the Colmans, the Cozens-Hardys, to mention only a handful, have always been great and zealous educators and philanthropists. So it was to be expected that Norwich would be the first provincial city, through the energy and foresight of Jeremiah James Colman, to accept the invitation and the challenge thrown out by the Trust's four founders and their supporters to call a public meeting, to set up a committee, and to open a school for girls in Norwich.

During its ninety-seven years of expanding life – there were 61 pupils when the school opened on 22 February 1875, and 681 in September 1971 – the school has occupied three places of singular distinction, even for Norwich which is a city of beautiful buildings. There is much to be said for going to school in a building or part of a building that has not been planned as a school, that suggests the intimacy of family or the gaiety of social life and retains something of the grace and dignity of a more leisured age. Each time our school has moved to surroundings that have given more opportunity for expansion it has inherited an atmosphere which has become part of its special 'flavour'. Two of its buildings were originally family houses; the third was an eighteenth-century Assembly House.

The family feeling must have surrounded the young school in its first two years at Churchman House, a handsome early georgian dwelling which had been occupied by successive generations of a family some of whose members had served the city as Mayor, Sheriff, and Aldermen. So from the beginning we stepped into a building that was linked with the proud civic life of Norwich. And we have never looked back – for from here in 1877 the school moved to the lovely georgian Assembly Rooms built by Thomas Ivory, one of the most inspired of eighteenth-century architects, and for the next fifty years or so the school went about its daily business in rooms that for beauty of proportion and exquisite craftsmanship have few equals anywhere. These rooms had been in their time the centre of the city's social life and in 1950, after being most beautifully restored, reverted once more to something of their original nature, becoming the focus for the musical and cultural activities of Norwich. And now, since 1933, we have occupied the third of our lovely buildings, an attractive regency house, cool and dignified and set in very beautiful and gracious gardens. This house, on to which the rest of the school buildings,

catching the lightness and loftiness of the original, have been most skil-
fully attached, had also been built as a home for his family by a distinguished Norwich citizen, Sir John Harrison Yallop, who was Mayor
more than once and Sheriff in 1805. As a house it must have been a satis-
fying place – and the sixth form, who now occupy its upper rooms as
a 'suite', and those who work in the library, once the dining room, can
look out on to the graceful slope of the front lawn, with its two magnificent
copper beeches at the far side and feel that they too are at home in surroundings that satisfy the senses and tranquillize the spirit. We have
become so used to calling our present senior school by the name it was
given when it was built as a private house in 1820 – Eaton Grove – that
it is only when we stop to consider what we shall put into an article of this
kind that we appreciate how very much its suggestion of leafiness and
lawns still remains true.

Over the past fourteen years we have acquired or had built for us more
space and more buildings. Lanchester House, a curious but interesting
edwardian family house with an attractive, irregular garden, conveniently
set on the edge of the Big Pitch, was bought for us by the Trust in 1957
and named after our then Chairman of Governors, Canon Lanchester.
It never houses fewer than 120 ten- to twelve-year-olds, and is set about
with music rooms too. Its acquisition, and the building of a caretaker's
house soon after, gave us more room at Eaton Grove for an additional
library called after Miss Jameson, headmistress from 1928 until 1946, and
for additional sixth-form rooms. We have two terrapin sixth-form laboratories which we could not do without and which seem to have acquired
a patina that makes them look not unattractive or incongruous alongside
the main school. Our magnificent gymnasium block was built in 1965
with very substantial and generous help from parents, and the Lanchester
House stables were converted into a sixth-form art and craft block in
1968, most of the painting and carpentry being done by girls and staff and
parents. There was a repeat performance of this kind of do-it-yourself
conversion at our junior school, Stafford House, about two years ago
when, mainly by self-help, a loft was converted into a very attractive
studio. The Trust has let us acquire the use of two large extra pieces of land
adjoining the school, one for lacrosse and rounders and the other for
athletics. So we have quite a kingdom on the Newmarket Road. But we
have not finished adding to it yet. In 1973 we shall begin to reorganize
ourselves, with a middle school to house 200 or so eight- to twelve-year-
olds, and the Trust is to build some exciting additions to Stafford House,
the present junior school. In the year of our own centenary, 1975, we are
to have a new laboratory block, to be built for us by the Trust, and we are
just about to embark on an appeal to parents, past and present, old girls
(and old boys!), and friends and well-wishers locally for funds to build still
more sixth-form accommodation – for our sixth form gets steadily larger,
and, who knows, if we raise enough, the swimming bath that comes up as
a regular suggestion at every meeting of the School Council.

Buildings do not make a school but give it something subtle, elusive,
but ineluctable. So it is perhaps from our three buildings with their

individual charm and their associations and from the spirit and character of those who caused them to be built that the school has acquired during its ninety-seven years of healthy existence what seem to have been, and seem still to be, its most striking characteristics. It has always had an appreciation of the city with its unbroken history as a flourishing centre of industry and culture, a city jealous, in the best sense of the word, to preserve itself and the unique county of which it is the 'capital' from too many disintegrating influences. I think it possible that Norwich High School has in it more daughters and grand-daughters, and great-grand-daughters of old girls than any other of the Trust schools. Its keen interest and continuous record of achievement in music, drama, and the other arts was perhaps fostered and matured by the half-century spent in the Assembly House. And might its sense of public service, shown not only in what it does, and has always done, to help causes both local and national, but also in the kind of careers which its members, past and present, have chosen or are choosing, have derived from those eminent and indefatigable citizens whose houses the school has occupied?

Nottingham

MISS L. L. LEWENZ, MA

Nottingham High School for Girls opened on 14 September 1875, in No. 1 Oxford Street. This house was abandoned five years later in favour of No. 9 Arboretum Street, the number of pupils having by then risen from the original 34 to almost 150. Considerably enlarged and altered, this house still forms the nucleus of the school's premises today, when numbers have gone up to over 900 and Nottingham is now the second largest school in the Trust, and the largest outside London.

Continuity is very much a feature of the school's history. Certain characteristics, which developed very early, have remained remarkably constant throughout the school's existence. As early as 1877, a society known as the 'Whetstone of Wit' was founded by a group of senior girls during fifth-form play time 'for the instruction and amusement of its members'. As well as holding regular meetings, it produced, unaided and by hand, a series of charming and unusual magazines, many of which survive to this day. Although the society eventually disappeared, the spirit of initiative and self-help survived, and remains a feature of the school now, as do also its clubs and societies.

Out-of-school activities were also provided by the staff from very early days. Although there was then no afternoon school, there was voluntary needlework on Tuesday afternoons (a tradition lasting over fifty years), botanical expeditions on Wednesdays – 'a wet Wednesday was a terrible disaster' – and cookery on Thursdays. Drill, taught by a master, tennis, later hockey and (surprisingly) football, wood carving, fretwork, and a debating society must have made life full and varied. A little later an annual Shakespeare competition was started. This dramatic competition has continued with few interruptions, except in wartime, until the present, though it is no longer confined to Shakespeare, and girls taking men's parts are no longer required to hide their lower limbs behind protective scenery or furniture. There were also a drill competition and a flower show, though these have not survived, and many expeditions were organized. Similar activities were arranged by the Old Girls' Association for its members, and although present-day old girls have too many other commitments to undertake a Reading Circle, or a series of lectures on 'Europe since Waterloo', the O.G.A. is surprisingly flourishing. It meets in London as well as Nottingham and its very successful ninety-fifth birthday party was attended by over 150 members.

Throughout its life the school has seen a constant extension of premises, which has never so far caught up with the expansion in numbers. The school's move to Arboretum Street was not an entirely adequate solution even from the start, as there was no assembly hall, and prayers had to be held in the vestibule. Even after a hall was provided, the accommodation must soon have seemed cramped as numbers continued to rise. Between 1921 and 1971 more houses were gradually acquired, until the school today occupies Nos. 9 to 27 inclusive and other properties are also in the Trust's possession. Not all these houses, however, were really suitable for school use; some had to be adapted or added to, and a few new buildings fitted in among them. One such scheme had just been started when war broke out in 1939, and building had to be abandoned in mid course, to be completed in 1947; but other improvements followed eventually, including the purchase of a church hall for use as a dining hall and the first stage of a purpose-built science wing. 1961 saw the beginning of a building fund which was started by the head girl and prefects. After ten years, and a special appeal launched in 1969, this fund totalled over £41,000, and building on the second and much larger stage of the science block began. This will be completed and officially opened during the Trust centenary year, and provides splendidly adequate accommodation for the very large numbers studying the sciences, as well as easing the pressures on other departments. The school's very restricted site has also created special difficulties in physical education. As long ago as 1878 a plea for better facilities had appeared in the 'Whetstone of Wit' under the pen name 'Illa Puella'. Her successors had to wait until 1933 for the gymnasium and until 1971 for the rowing which she specially craved. Tennis flourished in spite of difficulties, and in 1885 the tennis club challenged Sheffield to a tournament. The introduction of such activities as ice skating, squash, bowls, judo, and eventually rowing, for the sixth form, and swimming for the entire junior school and for upper thirds and lower fourths, have also helped considerably to satisfy the desire of 'illae puellae' today.

Perhaps our comparatively cramped quarters helped to maintain the unity of the school. In spite of its large numbers, Nottingham has never had a house system, and never wanted one. Even during the Second World War, when it was turned out of its buildings by the Army at twenty-four hours' notice and divided between three separate bases, the unity of the school was triumphantly maintained. So also were the numbers. The immediate postwar years found the upper school back in Arboretum Street, with a roofless hall, no heating system, no kitchen, and the younger girls still in temporary accommodation some miles away – but with numbers higher than ever, and the school ready to take up the challenge of the 1944 Education Act, and integrate the large numbers of pupils admitted from primary schools at the age of eleven under the new direct grant system.

It would be wrong to claim that this was done without any difficulties whatsoever, but that they were surmounted with comparative ease must have been largely due to the liberal outlook and approach which have always been strong in the school. In curriculum and teaching, the school has been forward-looking since Miss Skeel introduced book-keeping and social economy in the nineties. The combination of high academic standards with a flexibility which enable the most diverse individual needs and interests to be met were the guiding principles behind such policies as the maintenance of a strong home economics department, the introduction of pre-nursing and secretarial courses in the sixth and of current affairs throughout the upper school, the choice between French and German as a first foreign language, the abolition of streaming, and later the open sixth form and a tutorial system. 1945 saw the institution of a School Council, and the election of school officers began in 1948. In 1969 some joint teaching with the boys' High School sixth form was started and later extended; many joint social activities also flourish.

More important than curricula or organization is the spirit pervading them. It is quite certain that much of the quality and character of the school is due to a number of people who served it with devotion and discernment for a very long period of their lives. Professor Swinnerton, the first Chairman of the Local Governors, held this position from 1922 until his resignation in 1956, and his influence for good during such a long and formative period cannot be described adequately. Two other governors, Mrs Seely (an old girl) and Mr Stone, also served for over thirty years. Miss Hooke was secretary for thirty-five years. Mention must be made of Mr Edward Smith, caretaker from 1899 to 1935, and of his wife. Many of the teaching staff have given comparable or even longer service. There have been only four heads of the preparatory department in all: Miss Turner (1875-1901), Miss Anderson (1901-39), Miss Richards (1939-53, and on the staff from 1922), and the present junior school head, Miss Barnard. The school has had five remarkable headmistresses who have served it during most of its ninety-seven years. In 1883 Miss Skeel began her reign and imprinted much of herself on the school's development. A notable scholar, a commanding personality, and a woman of creative talent, she fostered all these qualities in others. She was followed in 1898 by Miss Clark, still remembered with affection by many old girls, and in 1921 by Miss Philipps, who had been on the staff since 1900 and served the school for thirty-five years in all before retiring after its diamond jubilee. Miss Philipps will also long be remembered, for her dignity (which never diminished her sense of humour) and for her gifts as a teacher. These two headships embraced almost four decades of growth combined with stability and continuity. But at the end of it the school was ready for a change, and Miss Merrifield brought a breath of fresh air and modernity, typified not only by the new uniform she introduced to rejoice the girls' hearts, but also by new courses and a new approach to the curriculum. Her headship covered the most difficult time in the school's history: the war years and the period of postwar reconstruction. Her devotion and resourcefulness were matched only by the clarity with which she set forth her principles, and the originality with which she applied them. Miss Milford succeeded in 1950, and managed to combine administrative skill with personal qualities which made her a guide, philosopher, and friend to countless pupils and colleagues. She enhanced the school's academic reputation and helped to safeguard its future development.

Finally, no history of the school would be complete without the names of such mistresses as Miss Barwood, Miss Pretty, Miss Ready, Miss Robinson, Miss Stainer, Miss Todd, Miss Tucker, and Miss Wootton, who all gave it long and devoted service. They, and many others whom it would be pleasant but impractical to name, did even more for the girls they worked with than to uphold traditions of scholarship: they displayed – and still do – in all their dealings, a spirit of kindness, generosity and sheer goodness, which must have influenced literally thousands in ways which history cannot record and which is a fundamental part of the greatness of the school.

Notting Hill & Ealing

MISS J. M. S. HENDRY, BA

In 1873 the newly formed Girls' Public Day School Company founded its first two schools, one at Kensington and one at Notting Hill, which in 1931 was transferred to Ealing and is now known as the Notting Hill & Ealing High School. Miss Harriet Morant Jones opened the school in Norland Square with ten girls; when she retired in 1900 it numbered more than 400. The buildings had been a boys' school: in the early years six classes at a time, divided by curtains, worked in the hall at the boys' ink-stained desks and benches. Miss Jones was a woman of outstanding ability and she attracted to her school a large number of exceptionally able mistresses and of unusually gifted pupils. Young teachers were encouraged to join her and stay for as much as a year before they became head-mistresses of the new girls' schools which were being founded very rapidly in the last decades of the nineteenth century. Her girls won sixty-five open scholarships to Cambridge, Oxford and London universities; many of her pupils achieved distinction in later life. In fact, such was its history at this remarkable period of its growth that it is not an exaggeration to say that the school made an outstanding contribution to the advance of higher education for women.

In the next thirty years, Miss Gavin, Miss Steele, Miss Paul, Miss Berryman, and Miss Oakden carried on the organization created by the founder and guided the school through the next stages of its development. During these years advanced courses in 'modern studies' and in science and mathematics were introduced: under Miss Berryman the older pupils were privileged to learn singing under the distinguished musician, Mr Charles Kennedy Scott.

Buildings were added, games fields were rented for hockey and cricket and the use of a field at Kensington Palace was granted by the Princess Louise. Physical education came into its own as a part of the curriculum. Unofficially, in a small paved yard at the back of the premises, seven-a-side 'hockey' was played with the feet and a small football, against a high wall, till the smashing of a window put a stop to what must have been an exciting game.

In 1930 Miss McCaig came as headmistress from Birkenhead and organized the removal of the school to its present home in the highest part of Ealing. To the original victorian house and an adjacent hall the Council added a large new wing. Old girls of the time tell of the delight of having gardens and tennis courts, of the anxious enthusiasm with which they waited for the workmen to finish the shining benches of the new laboratories and the pleasure of seeing the panelling from their former assembly hall re-erected (through the generosity of an old girl) in their new entrance hall, and their former sixth-form furniture installed in the new library together with J. J. Shannon's portrait of Miss Jones – one of the school's chief treasures. A few years later the original preparatory at Holland Park was closed and the under-elevens, grown too numerous by 1934 to be housed and taught in the main buildings, were transferred to Redlands in St Stephen's Road, Ealing. Through this addition to the premises more playing space became available: the school still lacks a playing field of its own but is fortunate in being able to rent part of a nearby athletic ground for hockey and tennis.

In 1936 the assembly hall, which although commodious was neither beautiful nor impressive, was completely transformed, the school by voluntary effort contributing nearly half the cost. In its new home the school was now stabilized; a large and responsible sixth form had emerged, after the first lean years following the move, when the top forms had been relatively small. The science work in the sixth form was developed to include preparation for a medical career, and as before a good proportion of girls went to the universities.

Both in their new and in their old home the girls established a fine tradition of social service; the Charity Society founded in 1899 was further developed, during the years that preceded the Second World War, by the work of a committee which represented each of the middle and senior forms.

During the war years the school remained open and admitted at the beginning a large number of girls as temporary transfers from other schools: at one time there were as many as nine different uniforms to be seen among the seniors. Redlands became a temporary boarding house and all girls were taught in the main buildings where the whole basement had been fortified with steel joists and bricked-up windows. Here, when necessary, lessons were taught, public examinations written, and the boarders slept. For one week this part of Ealing was without electricity so that life was carried on in the windowless shelters by the light of storm lanterns and candles. In the summer of 1944 both staff and girls were badly in need of rest and a number gratefully accepted the invitation of Sheffield High School to spend the summer holidays in its evacuation home in the country.

At the end of the war, as numbers further increased, Skipton House, next door to the main building, was bought by the Trust for the oldest of the junior forms. Premises were gradually restored and a new dining room formed out of a large army hut.

When Miss McCaig retired in 1950 the manifold tributes which poured in bore witness to the admiration and affection which she had inspired by her work, not only in combating so successfully the dangers and sorrows of the war but in passing on and enhancing the school's great tradition of intellectual achievement, personal responsibility, and service.

Miss Merrifield succeeded Miss McCaig and the school continued to expand and develop. A new physics laboratory and a music room were added and one of the outstanding events was the celebration of the eightieth birthday when old girls met for a great supper party and reminiscences. A large sum of money was raised to provide amenities for the school; an old girl, Lady Alexander of Tunis, gave the prizes; with a nice sense of fitness the sixth form had won six State Scholarships.

The next ten years saw many changes. New concepts of the nature of state education and the spread of comprehensive schools brought uncertainty for the direct grant schools. The disappearance of the Middlesex Education Authority meant that the school now drew its pupils from seven different Local Authorities. It was with sadness and dismay that the Trust learned of the decision of Ealing Education Authority not to take up places in the school from 1966. In 1968, following a great effort by the Trust and a splendid body of parents, the decision was rescinded, but has been reinstated for 1972. All the other authorities have happily maintained their links with the school.

Parents and old girls showed the strength of their support in other ways. At the ninetieth birthday in 1963 an appeal was launched for funds for a new library – which was to be opened in our centenary year in 1973. The fund progressed so joyously and was invested so wisely by the excellent administrative committee of parents and staff that the library was built and opened by Dame Kitty Anderson three years early, in 1970. The Trust generously added £7,000 to the £15,000 raised and the new building on Skipton lawn also provides excellent sixth-form accommodation. It is hoped to landscape the ground round the new building in memory of Miss McCaig.

The school continues to flourish in other ways. A steadily increasing number of girls go on to university and other places of higher education. The Charity Society has given place to the Social Services Committee and much active practical help is offered in the neighbourhood, in addition to the vigorous fund raising which supports a wide variety of good causes. The prefect system ended several years ago and the sixth form no longer wear uniform. Many school expeditions, field courses, journeys abroad, educational cruises, widen the horizons of the girls and the teaching takes full advantage of modern equipment, so that the school has television, radio, tape-recorders, and other aids to learning and understanding.

The next great event, apart from the Trust's centenary in 1972, will be the school's own centenary in 1973 and that will be very properly and merrily celebrated.

TOPICS DEBATED IN THE SCHOOLS

1890   *That coeducation is desirable.*

1901   *That the decay of manners is to be deplored.*

1901   *That conformity to fashion in dress is desirable.*

1904   *That prizes and marks are more harmful than helpful.*

1934   *Little girls should be seen and not heard.*

Oxford

MRS H. M. WARNOCK, MA, BPhil

On 3 November 1875, twenty-nine girls assembled at the Judge's Lodgings for the first day of a new school. Miss Ada Benson, a formidable lady and a sister of the future Archbishop of Canterbury, was their headmistress, and she had three assistants. Almost immediately, there begin to appear on the roll the names of families who were famous in Oxford, and who were to become in some sense the founders of the school. Among the very first pupils were three Max Müller sisters, three Mayhew sisters, no less than nine Underhills, sisters and cousins. There were Ethel and Julia Arnold, the nieces of Matthew Arnold, the latter of whom became Mrs Leonard Huxley, herself the founder of Prior's Field School for girls, where, with characteristic courage, she gave her sons Aldous and Julian their early education. A little later, there appear six Vernon Harcourt sisters, who used to bicycle in line on boys' machines to St Giles from Cowley Grange, where their father, a student of Christ Church, used to live. The famous Spooner of New College sent his daughter to us in 1890, and A. L. Smith of Balliol sent all but one of his numerous and brilliant daughters to the school (and one of them, Rosalind Clay, is still teaching history for us, to a privileged few college entrance candidates).

The school, it can be seen, benefited greatly from the relatively new phenomenon of married fellows of colleges, and our history is tied up inevitably with the Betjeman-loved history of North Oxford, as our pupils' address book will verify – Bradmore Road, Norham Gardens, Norham End, Crick Road, Fyfield Road, Warnborough Road, Park Terrace – they all appear and reappear. The city and the university, the professions and trades, are equally represented.

It is hard not to linger over this period of the school's history. It would be lovely to know more, for instance, of Letitia Bawden from Museum Road, who was 'removed by her mother's wish for bad conduct at home', or of Alexandra Kitchin who left after less than a year, in 1876, 'on account of obstinacy'. But we must move on.

The first number of the school magazine appeared four years after the founding of the school. 'Many girls', we read, 'put on their gloves in the street, and some wear *no* gloves going to and from school. The latter I have heard objected to more than anything and it certainly gives our enemies reason to say that the High School makes girls rough and unfeminine.' And again: 'A great deal could be done if only a few girls would bind themselves together to uphold the honour of the form, to shun anything underhand as beneath them, to work conscientiously, and to speak out boldly. Are there none who will do this?' At the same time work was proceeding and some of it must have been taxing and stimulating, as when the Revd. C. H. Dodgson came up from Christ Church to teach logic to the fifth form. And in 1883 Miss Bishop allowed a violin class to be started, experimentally, in the summer term, for present and old pupils together, and later in the term she gave a musical party, at which they played, among other items, a whole Haydn symphony (how scored, one longs to know).

In 1880 the school moved to 21 Banbury Road, where it stayed under successive headmistresses – Miss Bishop, Miss Soulsby, Miss Leahy, Miss Haig Brown, Miss Gale, Miss Stack – until the great day in 1957 when it moved to new buildings in Belbroughton Road. Much of the early history of the school consists, necessarily, of the battle for the recognition of women's education, and its defence against attack. The battle being fought in the universities was being fought in the schools at the same time, and again and again the same note is sounded. 'At present we must own', writes a contributor to the magazine, 'that we are physically very much inferior to men. But must this always be so? Would it not be possible to give women sports and outdoor exercise of every kind, so that their bodies may be strengthened while they are working hard with their brains?' Or this desperate cry: 'There is nothing nobler than a true mother or a true wife. But at the same time we must remember that all women *cannot* marry, and, therefore, what must be done with the remainder?' But gradually, through the years, the battle has been mostly won, and the tone becomes less anxious and justificatory, and more straightforwardly confident. We began to know, and not to need to say, that what we and all the Trust schools were doing was worth doing, and was appreciated.

Now, in 1972, the Belbroughton Road site is at last compact. The junior school (which now begins at age nine) and the boarding house are all together. We are hemmed in by a new major road, and new city schools, but we feel ourselves, perhaps partly because of this, to be a unity. Through the generosity of parents and friends of the school, we have a swimming pool and a sixth-form common room. We hope soon to appeal to them yet again for a music block.

The academic achievements of the school are very great; its musical achievements quite as remarkable. Art and drama flourish. The universities are scattered with former members of the school, the local orchestras and choirs with present members. But the one question one may raise, knowing all these facts, is what is it actually *like* to be at the Oxford High School now? And of course we who are here find it hardest to answer this question. Our greatest link with the past is our continued close connection with the city and university. The greatest difference is perhaps in what we say to, and about, ourselves. When the school began, it was considered appropriate for the headmistress to express the aims of the school in terms which seem to us to reach the extremes of sententiousness – to harangue the pupils every term about duty and bearing and the consolations of religion, as well as about the moral shabbiness of *passing notes*, a vice much mentioned as late as the thirties. The distance between the headmistress and the school seems immense; moral clichés, now too embarrassing to repeat, abound in speeches and talks. Nowadays I believe

DEIRDRE by Epstein, gift of The Friends of the GPDST.

that our aims are just as serious, and certainly just as valuable, but we are far more ready to believe that our pupils make their own choices and seek out their own enthusiasms. Quite simply, for good or ill, we trust them more. The feeling of co-operation in a common aim is one of the greatest pleasures of school; and on the whole the common aim can be assumed. The values of independent thought and hard work are those which we would be prepared to state most openly. If, in the course of duty, we storm at people for leaving their possessions around, or for leaving school before the bell goes, we do not turn this into a moral issue; the role of the homily is far less, but it would be quite misleading to argue from this that the tone is lower. It is just different. It is less acceptable than it was to talk about morality and more important than ever to be clear about what, in school life, is trivial and temporary and what is, as we hope, a real and true foundation for life.

Portsmouth

MISS M. L. CLARKE, MA, ARCM, GRSM

Portsmouth in the eighteen seventies provided 'Educational Establishments for Young Ladies', but these combined poor teaching with social pretensions, and businessmen's daughters were not acceptable. In 1881 a group of prominent citizens, led by Canon Grant, the Vicar of Portsmouth, approached the Girls' Public Day School Company for advice on remedying this situation. Things moved fast; by July, 560 of the Company's shares had been bought, Marlborough House in Osborne Road secured, and Miss Ledger, of the Mary Datchelor School, appointed headmistress, and in February 1882 Portsmouth High School was opened. Miss Ledger succeeded in gaining the support of both naval and townspeople, and the new school grew rapidly. Academic standards improved, and by the end of 1882, numbers having risen from thirty to a hundred, Burlington House next door was acquired. In September 1885 the school moved to its present building (described at that time as 'convenient and suitable'), which was officially opened the following February by Princess Louise, on the occasion of the prizegiving. The headmistress's report (read by the Chairman of the Local Committee) stated: 'Miss Ledger is entirely satisfied with the conduct of her pupils, and in a large majority of cases, with their work.' Her optimism was justified when eight years later, a High School girl, Lily Flowers, was the first Portsmouth woman to go to university. The school continued to expand; the preparatory department opened in 1889, the kindergarten the following year, and the first official boarding house in 1900. Both staff and girls recognized Miss Ledger's qualities of tact and charm; standards of ladylike behaviour might be exacting, but in the words of a pupil, 'she gave us a love of truth, honesty, courtesy and the gracious things of life'.

In 1900 Miss Ledger retired, owing to ill health, and was replaced by Miss Adamson, an energetic and practical administrator. An old girl of Notting Hill High School and a physics scholar of Bedford College, she vigorously brought the school into the twentieth century, with up-to-date teaching methods, sterner academic demands, team games, and greater emphasis on social service; and to her we owe the founding of the school magazine. Unfortunately, Miss Adamson too had to retire for health reasons, and her successor, Miss Steele (1905–8), was soon transferred to Notting Hill.

This period of rapid change was followed by one of continuity, when Miss Cossey came to Portsmouth from Croydon High School, staying until the school's golden jubilee in 1932. During Miss Cossey's years of office, numbers rose from under 200 to 360, the new block containing a reference library, laboratory, and two formrooms was opened in 1926, and the junior school moved to Dovercourt in 1928. Under her, many of the school's lasting traditions were founded, and a lively and adventurous spirit was encouraged. Games, music, social services, and the Old Girls' Guild all flourished, and present and former pupils gained outstanding successes in many fields. For the first time, there were open scholarships to Cambridge and London colleges, and old girls went on to distinguished careers in the artistic and academic worlds. Miss Cossey's long reign fittingly ended with the school's jubilee in 1932. During this splendid year, two girls gained open scholarships to Cambridge and the Jubilee Fund reached nearly £1,200. Dr Lang, Archbishop of Canterbury, and Dr Garbett, future Archbishop of York – both former Chairmen of the Local Committee – were among many who sent tributes and congratulations. In many generations of pupils, Miss Cossey had fostered those ideals which she quoted at her first prizegiving, 'childlike faith, intellectual reverence, and not the least, gaiety and cheerfulness of aim'.

Miss Cossey's successor, Miss Watt, came from St Paul's Girls' School. As a historian, she foresaw and prepared for the coming emergency. In September 1939 Portsmouth High School was evacuated to two pleasant country houses thirteen miles apart, Adhurst St Mary and Hinton Ampner, and overnight became a boarding school, only 200 strong. This episode, a history in itself, is too complex to be described in this short account.

In 1941 Miss Watt left for St Swithun's, Winchester, and Miss Thorn, already head of the mathematics staff, became headmistress. To her fell the formidable task of postwar reconstruction. In 1945 came the return to Southsea, to a building battered by such wartime vicissitudes as occupation by the Army and the WRNS, and high explosive and incendiary bombs. Under Miss Thorn's dauntless leadership, life returned to normal; the school gradually reassembled, traces of occupation were removed, and the boarders moved into Dovercourt and School House (which had been bought in 1934). Then began a period of great expansion, social, physical, intellectual. By 1959 the school numbered nearly six hundred, with a sixth form of a hundred or more, a size which it still maintains, in spite of the closure of the boarding house in 1953. Miss Thorn was not afraid of innovation; uniform was modernized, the Parent Staff Association founded, and latterly, formal prizegivings were abolished and prefects were given an attractive common room. Horizons were widened by school journeys at home and abroad, including contacts with Southampton University, Slapton Ley Field Centre, and the Luisenschule in Mulheim. Accommodation was gradually expanded to cope with the population explosion; playground and cloakroom space was enlarged and the physics laboratory and a former domestic science kitchen at Dovercourt were remodelled. In 1955 came the new wing, providing a dining room, a modern chemistry laboratory, and two formrooms, and new blocks appeared at Dovercourt in 1957, and at the main school eight years later. On the teaching side, staff were always encouraged to introduce fresh ideas (for example, this school was a pioneer in the Cambridge Classics Project) and more and more girls embarked on ambitious careers and gained academic distinction. In 1968, the year of Miss Thorn's retirement, twenty-three girls went up to university, there were two student scholarships and one entrance scholarship, and three old girls came top of their year – a fitting crown to a great epoch.

Today, true to its history, the school continues to keep abreast of the times, with new approaches to subjects, wider syllabuses and the abolition of uniform in the sixth form. On the building side, we are facing exciting new developments. We have recently acquired an overflow laboratory, and by 1974 the Trust has generously promised us a splendid new science-cum-art block, which will free much needed extra space elsewhere.

Portsmouth High School has served this city and district well for ninety years, and has a firm place in the affections of many. To quote M. E. Howell's words concerning our 75th anniversary: 'Its history has been one of growth and new life – and the story still goes on.'

Putney

MISS R. SMITH, BA

A growth in population from 54 to 670; five scattered houses until the final acquisition of the site on Putney Hill in 1918; the service of seven headmistresses, this is the history of Putney High School during the seventy-eight years of its life.

Founded in 1893, it was the thirty-fifth school of the Trust. The Girls' Public Day School Company, as it was then, provided a school only when it was asked for by people living in the locality. At that time there was only one girls' school in Putney and when parents applied for a GPDSC school to be opened in the neighbourhood, Mary Gurney, a local resident and one of the great pioneers of women's education, supported the application. Burlington House, in the Upper Richmond Road, was leased for the East Putney High School and twenty-seven local girls who already attended Wimbledon High School, founded thirteen years before, transferred to this new school on their doorstep. Miss S. M. Huckwell was brought from Liverpool High School to be the first headmistress.

As the popularity of the school grew, additional premises were acquired: first Albert House, on the opposite side of Upper Richmond Road, and, when Burlington House was considered unsafe owing to soil subsidence and had to be vacated, No. 18 Carlton Road. At first lessons were held only in the morning, for in those days girls were considered delicate creatures, scarcely able to survive the rigours of a full scholastic day. Special tuition in music and drawing was given in the afternoon, however, and pupils were allowed to attend between 2.30 and 4.00 p.m. 'to be assisted by the teachers to prepare their lessons'.

In spite of their presumed frailty, the girls were encouraged to take exercise. An army sergeant took them for drill and gymnastics in a hall in Wandsworth. Tennis was played on an asphalt court at Albert House presented by Mary Gurney, and later hockey, rounders, and athletics were introduced.

After seven years Miss Huckwell left to be married and Miss Edith Major came from Blackheath High School where she had been an assistant mistress, to become head of a flourishing school of over a hundred girls.

Miss Major's outstanding qualities were her wit and scholarship. With the first she enlivened the school and endeared herself to staff and pupils; the second inspired the intellectual effort and enthusiasm which brought academic successes to Putney's university entrants.

Numbers continued to rise and an attempt was made to obtain larger premises. It was felt that Putney Hill would be the most desirable site. In 1906, Homefield, No. 37 Putney Hill, was bought. It was adapted and opened in 1910 as the new junior school. In the same year Miss Major was appointed headmistress of King Edward VI High School for Girls, Birmingham. She was a leading figure in the world of education and when she became Mistress of Girton received one of its highest awards.

Putney's third headmistress was Miss Ruth Hewetson who had been on the staff of Liverpool High School. She was the creator of the school as it stands today. She had a passion for buildings and at once made plans to have the whole school on one site. Largely through her vision and enterprise, the Council decided to buy Cromwell Lodge, the house next to Homefield on Putney Hill, and add an assembly hall, a laboratory, and a covered way between the houses. The old stable was converted into a studio by a gift from the Old Girls' Association, and in the summer of 1915 the house in Carlton Road was sold and the whole school was together on Putney Hill. Three years later, Lytton House, whose grounds adjoin those of Homefield, also fell vacant and became the junior school and a year after that a concrete prefabricated building – a relic of the First World War known to generations of Putney girls as the 'Huts' – was bought from the Government and added to the east end of the hall. When Miss Hewetson left in 1920 to become one of His Majesty's Inspectors it was with the knowledge that her dream of making the school a unity had been achieved.

Three years after Miss M. G. Beard had taken Miss Hewetson's place numbers had risen to 450 and a new building programme was drawn up. A long corridor was continued south from the 'Huts', with music rooms and cloakrooms on one side and laboratories on the other, and a large new gymnasium was built at the end.

Through Miss Beard's influence the school developed in new directions. Art, history, and gramophone clubs, and a dramatic society were founded. A most ambitious 'Pageant of London' was held in the school grounds, attended by over 1,400 people. And for almost the first time the staff began to travel abroad and make exchanges with the staffs of schools in different parts of the world. It was a time of expansion and adventure and under Miss Beard's guidance the school flourished academically, athletically, culturally, and socially. Until this time the school emblem had been the violet. Miss Beard changed this to the more robust oak tree, but retained purple as the school's colour.

Miss K. E. Chester, who took Miss Beard's place in 1930, had the longest reign of any of Putney's headmistresses, and the most difficult since she was responsible for the school through the years of the Second World War. Before the outbreak of war she had done much to foster a social sense among her pupils; she had encouraged them to work for local and national charities and particularly for the Union of Girls' Schools Settlement at Peckham. She also gave support to the many clubs and societies started in Miss Beard's time and initiated others.

When war broke out, the Metropolitan Police arrived to take possession of the school buildings; those of the school who agreed to go were evacuated to Queen Anne's, Caversham. Throughout the first years of the war the school was divided between Putney and Caversham and Miss Chester spent part of every week at Caversham. Early in 1941 she brought news that the house next to Cromwell Lodge had been completely demolished by a direct hit. 'The police officials who were in the hall when the bomb fell', says Miss Chester, 'told me that the roof rose about six inches and then, in keeping with our best traditions, quietly settled into its place again as though nothing unusual had occurred.'

Miss Chester remained at Putney for five years after the end of the war and was able to see the school re-established. When she retired in 1950 she was followed by Miss K. Lockley who came from the headship of Brighton & Hove High School and had before that been on the staff of Putney. New buildings were begun soon after her arrival. First the old studio was demolished and rebuilt, then a large room outside the hall was turned into a library, and a little later two new classrooms and additional cloakroom accommodation were added to the west side of the 'Huts' corridor.

Most enterprising and imaginative of all Miss Lockley's many activities was the launching of a building fund appeal in November 1959, to pay for new sixth-form rooms to be erected over the newly built classrooms. Staff, school, old girls, parents, and friends responded generously, and within eighteen months over £5,000 had been subscribed. The appeal culminated in a gigantic fête which raised over £3,000 in one afternoon, and in January 1962 the sixth form moved into their new rooms.

It is now over eight years since Miss Lockley's retirement. Putney's external appearance, with its spread of buildings and pleasant and spacious grounds, has remained the same apart from the addition of a cedarwood classroom block built beside the pond. In minor matters the school has changed, sensitive as a living community must be to the changes outside. No longer are there the formalities of prizegivings, the rivalry of 'houses'. Open days now show something of the school's achievements in its many and varied activities; junior clubs provide opportunities for older girls to help the younger and a School Society enables all voices to be heard. Trouser suits have a place on the uniform list and the sixth form are free to wear what they like. They are given freedom too in their choice of physical activities; they may fence, play squash or golf, ice-skate, or trampoline as well as take part, if they wish, in team games. These are superficial changes; in major matters, in the desire to use abilities fully and vitally, in concern for other people and appreciation of their gifts, in responsiveness to need or an occasion, the school does not change.

Eight years ago the Council bought a plot of land adjoining the school and this purchase now makes it possible to plan confidently for the future. By the beginning of the next academic year the junior school will have three new formrooms and in the following year a science block is to be built. Over £4,000 has been raised by parents, staff, friends, and past and present girls to help with these buildings, a proof of the continuing care and generosity which Putney evokes.

Sheffield

MISS M. C. LUTZ, MA

'From the first the school seemed to spring into vigorous life', writes an anonymous contributor to the first school magazine, published a decade after thirty-nine girls had assembled in Sheffield's Music Room for the opening of the school in March 1878. Ten years later over 350 girls worked and played in their 'new and handsome building in Rutland Park', which had been completed in 1884 and had 'the special advantages of a studio, a gymnasium and a playground, including a tennis court'.

The great Mrs Woodhouse was to all intents and purposes the first head-mistress and we owe her a tremendous debt, not only for an attractive building equipped with facilities which must have seemed extravagant and eccentric in her day, but above all for acquiring a site in the green and pleasant surroundings of Broomhill. In 1895 the Secondary Education Commission made special mention of 'the fine building, surrounded by charming grounds . . . inside perfectly efficient as a school building, and yet there is no stiffness and formality about it, and while every classroom is different from the next, yet every classroom has a charm of its own'. In 1972 those charms have to make up for some inconvenience because of our increased numbers, but we are fortunate in some recent acquisitions: for example an attractive house at the bottom of our garden, whose charming eccentricities have been ingeniously adapted to the teaching of modern languages. French and German have always flourished in the school and in 1972 the first party of linguists will be visiting Russia.

The school's greatest pride in 1884 was the new gymnasium which enabled it to become one of the first Trust schools to introduce regular physical work (and with it medical inspections). The magazine waxes lyrical about the gymnasium – 'we find that enthusiasm . . . for active exercises is shown by the intellectually vigorous' – and welcomes the healthier style of dress 'whose comfort and convenience will allow of the easy and graceful movement of the whole body'. Quoting Charles Kingsley, the author declares war on 'the three most common causes of ill-filled lungs in children . . . stillness, silence and stays'.

This year the original gymnasium has been turned into a sixth-form study and common room – the grey tiles with their blue and yellow striped dado have been painted over in more modern hues but we cherish the centre pillars, memorials of that drill sergeant of 1884 who was soon replaced by fully trained gymnasts. Their ghosts no doubt preside approvingly over the miniskirted upper sixths and the complete absence of stays, stillness, and silence in their common room. Mrs Woodhouse would, surely, have been overjoyed to see our new gymnasium – a lofty Congregational church, built of local sandstone a century ago close to our grounds and now converted by the Trust's architect into a superb gymnasium, complete with trampoline which will take the most athletic a little closer to the neo-gothic roof. The size of the nave allows us to play all the winter games indoors with space for two badminton courts – and room for table tennis in the side aisles. As yet we find it somewhat unnerving to have so much space to run about in – and to make a noise in church! The same does not apply to the semi-basements where spacious cloakrooms, footbaths, and showers inspire less reverence.

Games have always flourished, especially tennis. The great adventure of the eighteen-eighties was a trip to Nottingham to compete for an old tennis racquet (in the last ten years this same racquet has become the senior trophy in the Northern Trust Schools' Rally); in 1970 for the third year running we represented the North of England in the final of the Aberdare Cup (open to all schools) and came second. Alas, we no longer flood the tennis courts for skating as did earlier and tougher generations – nor do we any longer provide cocoa at the Olympic-sized swimming baths which the university now kindly lend us for our weekly lessons. In recent years, several girls have swum for city and county and one girl has represented Great Britain.

In 1895 the commissioners reported critically on 'a very small laboratory, but though of a poor kind, some of the girls seem to manage to do a little practical botany, chemistry and work with the microscope' – little did they know that the microscopes were borrowed from local doctors! Even so, many girls distinguished themselves in the Natural Sciences Tripos, especially in medicine, and Helen Wilson became not only the first woman doctor in Sheffield but also well known internationally for pioneering work in preventive and social medicine. We acquired a laboratory block in 1961, and last year converted two further rooms into laboratories to meet the growing demand. Geology has also been introduced in the last decade; our predecessors pursued the subject as a club activity and even engaged in regular field work. There has always been a strong mathematical tradition in the school and today every girl studies some aspect of the subject for two years beyond O Level.

In the last twenty years or so there has been a remarkable development in the breadth and depth of academic work – New Testament Greek, language orals on tape – much of it aided and encouraged by the often maligned Joint Matriculation Board. Even if there was no manufacture of slab pots eighty years ago, there were surprisingly enlightened opportunities for artistic self-expression. The school's excellent musical work which still leads to first-class concerts and close co-operation with the music department of the university was started by Miss Froebel, a pupil of Madame Schumann, who introduced men and women of international repute to set the school the highest standards. In art, too, much interesting and adventurous work has always been done; in 1893 the school was gaining awards for its work at the Chicago Exhibition, in 1971 all the work sent in for a children's art exhibition was accepted by the Graves Art Gallery.

Links with the university have been very close and the excellent Teacher

Training Department attached to the school from its foundation became a part of the university in 1922. The school's outstanding academic achievements are a tradition frequently remarked upon by inspectors and academics. On a unique occasion in 1965, HM Inspectors had the pleasure of attending Advanced Level lessons given by the Professor of Physics who had kindly stepped into the breach when the physics specialist left suddenly. It was felt that the school had surpassed itself. . . . In 1895 it was reported that girls usually attended the school from the kindergarten to the age of eighteen or nineteen and that seven or eight girls went on to Oxford or Cambridge every year. Nowadays it is most unusual for any girl to leave before finishing the A level courses and, while the average number of Oxford and Cambridge entrants has remained very much the same since 1895, it is encouraging that the number of girls going on to universities has risen from thirteen in 1961 to forty-seven in 1971.

Nine decades have seen interesting changes in the staffing of the school, especially since the war. From the start, Mrs Woodhouse set very high standards of academic and professional qualifications for her staff, although she herself was entirely self-educated. As soon as they became available, she engaged graduates and the tributes paid to these dedicated women and their successors show not only that they gave exceptionally long and devoted service to the school but also that many played leading parts in various activities outside it. In 1972 twenty-five out of forty members of staff are married women (ten years ago there were six) – and two are men. The number of part-time staff has doubled during the same period and we have learnt to appreciate the more detached contribution which these ladies have to make. Inevitably, extra-curricular activities are somewhat curtailed, but staff and girls who in prewar days would have lived only for the school and devoted all their more ample spare time to it, now do social work in the city, play in local orchestras, teams, and amateur drama and opera, sing in mixed choirs, run clubs, and teach in Sunday school.

It is interesting that the earliest generations were much concerned, not with the school's reputation as a ladylike establishment but with the service it gave to the community and the use its members made of their rich opportunities. It is perhaps the sharing in external activities that enables the present generation to establish a friendly relationship with the staff, based on natural courtesy and a mutual respect for effort and achievement.

School societies, however, still flourish and are well if selectively supported. School plays, for nearly half a century most expertly produced by Miss Taylor and Miss Outram, herself a very early pupil of the school, are still an eagerly awaited event, and opera is now included in the repertoire. Debating societies, in existence since 1884, now compete in university sponsored competitions with considerable success in the final rounds.

We retain the four 'houses' named after the Trust's founders whose portraits, flanked by those of former headmistresses, are studied with considerable interest (and some frivolity) by all who pass along the middle corridor. A few years ago a public debate on a motion to abolish the houses revealed a sincere attachment to them and a mature appreciation of the part they play in dividing the school vertically and providing opportunities for leadership and co-operation to many who would not otherwise be able to contribute of their gifts. With unusual historical sense and delightful wit we were told that the houses are not just links with the Trust's past but part of the family history of a large number of girls in the school whose grandmothers and great grandfathers had worn the colours of the house in which present members hoped to see their own daughters.

When the school moved to Rutland Park the junior department shared the new building with the older girls, but in 1917 the Council bought Moor Lodge, which had been the manor house of Broomhill. It is a delightful house, bright and cheerful with its high, ornate ceilings and large windows looking out over the garden where the children can play – and hide. There is a naturally happy, homely atmosphere which immediately strikes all our visitors. When the war came and the school miraculously adapted itself to boarding life in a Methodist lay preachers' training college in Derbyshire, not even the delights of being bathed by the staff, making gas masks for one's teddy bear, and ploughing through more than a foot of snow in the middle of the Peak district, made up for memories of Moor Lodge. From the earliest days, senior girls were encouraged to take an interest in the junior department, especially if they wanted to teach.

In 1965 we launched our first major appeal for building funds since the school was founded. The response was most generous and within a year a superb extension had been added to the Woodhouse Memorial Library, which was far too small for a senior school of 430 girls (the 160 juniors have their own library). We can now house reference and fiction libraries, careers pamphlets, magazines, and art and record collections in one room and we have allowed for future expansion – a change from 1889 when the school magazine appealed to old girls to lend books for a term or longer to supplement the school's meagre resources.

In 1889 an anonymous writer in the first magazine presents 'a peaceful record of work done, examinations passed, of efforts to help others' and she paints a picture of girls grave and gay, singleminded but capable of enjoying a good laugh, affectionately proud of their school but not beyond having a little giggle over the idiosyncrasies of some of 'the mistresses', very seriously concerned over social injustices but delightfully content to 'enjoy themselves in a leisurely manner'. To a historian, these records are an unending source of pleasure and comfort for they show that the contemporaries of Miss Beale and Miss Buss were very much like us in the things that really matter. We still have the 'Cot Fund' which they started and our annual contribution to world-wide as well as local charities amounts to well over £250 every year; but we must not forget that several of our early old girls gave their lives in the mission field while others died of diseases contracted through work done in the slums of the great cities. Practical help in the city's less privileged areas, even 'Play Projects', are not the prerogatives of our decade since the school sponsored similar projects in pre-1914 days.

Sheffield: DAME KITTY ANDERSON in the library extension she opened in 1966

The last ten years have seen the introduction of harvest festivals to help the aged and infirm in the city, new and interesting experiments in morning assembly and carol services, regular parents' meetings, health education, the use of television and other audio-visual aids, consultative committees, new style school meals, and occasional 'open days' to replace regular prizegivings. We were amongst the first schools to abolish prefects and probably amongst the last to see the disappearance of hut classrooms erected as temporary buildings in 1918, complete with eccentric stoves which should have been disposed of as valuable antiques. There has also been some decline in support for the Old Girls' Association, partly owing to the greater mobility of the population and partly because old girls rightly have wider interests. The past decade has seen the increase in expeditions beyond the city boundaries and across the Channel.

Girls of today share with their predecessors an irrepressible gaiety, a delight in using all their faculties. Though our skirts may be getting longer, we are not at pains to conceal our blue (albeit brown) stockings. Uniform is the subject of careful discussion, and retained as an important means of obliterating social and economic differences.

The fact that the school offers its form of education to the community as a whole has always been a great strength. One of the 1895 commissioners remarks: 'The Headmistress . . . is one of the very few I have met who is not afraid to mix girls of different social positions in her school', and the Report pleads for 'the development of something like a complete system which will enable every child in Sheffield . . . and those of special ability in special lines to have the door opened to them, from whatever class they may come.' The same plea was made to the Sheffield Education Authority in 1969, when after forty years of most successful co-operation it decided to sever its links with the school. Since then appreciation of the aims and methods of the school has not diminished, and applications for Governors' free places and for assisted fee-paying places come from all parts of the city and the two neighbouring counties. In the past, in the twenties and thirties and the war years, we may have had girls of a far wider range of ability, but probably not from such a variety of family backgrounds. We in fact now serve a very wide area, both rural and industrial, and form a community of versatile talents to which all can contribute, with no one debarred through parents' inability to pay fees – or to buy a house in a specific catchment area.

Our founders, many of whose descendants have been connected with the school as governors, benefactors, parents, and pupils, showed York-shire shrewdness and foresight in building a school which has stood the test of time. While Sheffield is proud to belong to the family of the GPDST, it has a distinctive character and a healthy independence which spring from its deep local roots.

Shrewsbury

MISS M. CRANE, BA

Shrewsbury High School opened on 5 May 1885, with thirty-one girls in
the senior school, nineteen juniors being admitted a week later. It began
its existence at Clive House in College Hill which the first headmistress,
Miss Edith Cannings (promoted from the staff of Croydon High School),
describes as a beautiful old house with oak floors and oak panelled walls.
Not surprisingly the growing young school soon demanded more space
and in 1886 the new 'Iron House', disrespectfully known as 'The Tin
Tabernacle' was erected in the grounds and used for prayers, art, and singing lessons.

By no means all public opinion in Shrewsbury at that time approved
the ideals on which the school was founded. There were those who felt
that scripture could not properly be taught in an undenominational
school, and it is clear from the comments of eminent local persons at early
prizegivings that many doubted the wisdom of trying to impart academic
education to girls.

Nevertheless, expansion continued, and 105 pupils in 1897 transferred
from Clive House to the grand new building on Murivance. Early in 1898
the Princess Louise performed the opening ceremony, an occasion
vividly described in the local paper. The work had cost *nine thousand
pounds!* And it was noted with particular admiration that 'the assembly
hall and some of the rooms are warmed by hot water'. Whatever short-
comings present generations may find in the site and building, the girls
of that era were enchanted by the elegant new hall with its pillars, gallery,
and honours boards, and with the spacious grounds and gardens.

In so brief an account not much can be said about changes in the curriculum over the years, but certain developments and characteristics stand
out. From copies of early time-tables we find there was, even then, a bias
towards languages, for which the school later became well known.
Included were Latin, German, French, and a number of approaches to
the native tongue, viz. reading, writing, dictation, composition, repeti-
tion, and literature. Grammar and mathematics appear in 1886 and in
1892 there is reference to statics and dynamics! Botany and geography
were taught from the beginning but the serious development of science
had to wait until after the Second World War. In the early years geography
remained a Cinderella subject, but history was generally to the fore, and
in the thirties we find appreciative references to current events lessons and
a civics course embracing expeditions and 'environmental studies'. From
the beginning the school was fortunate in the remarkable and often distinguished men and women who encouraged its music and art, and
physical education has been undiminished in popularity and standard of

work. Domestic subjects however, have not been popular and sporadic attempts to encourage 'the home arts' appear to have withered away very quickly.

The advent of the Priory Girls' Grammar School in 1911 checked the rise in numbers temporarily, but the need for more facilities continued. Various alterations and additions were made within the main building and in 1924 a new art studio was built in the grounds. In 1935, the year of the school's golden jubilee and the retirement of Miss Gale, a beautiful new library leading from the assembly hall was provided by past and present members of the school. More prosaically, in 1948 Miss Hudson, whose period of headship coincided with the war and the restrictions and shortages of the following decade, was able to announce in the school magazine the completion of the canteen kitchen – a significant feature in the amenities of SHS where healthy appetites abound and many have to make long journeys to school. The same year saw the return of the hockey field (sacrificed as part of the school's war effort), and the construction of two new tennis courts.

From the beginning the junior school has been an important part of the school. At first housed in the main school, in 1932 it moved, with its sixty pupils, to its own specially acquired premises next door, Hampden House. In 1959 the Trust purchased Stepping Stones, a preparatory school in Kennedy Road and, joined by a number of its pupils, the junior school moved once more. In 1960 two fine modern classrooms were added and a delightful hall with canteen facilities fashioned from an old coach house and outbuildings. The juniors have spacious gardens and play areas in this quiet residential area, though we in the senior school often wish the distance a little less and opportunities to be with them more frequent. A sad feature of the early sixties was the departure from the junior house of the little boys. Small boys had always been admitted hitherto and many a solid Salopian can claim to be an old boy of the High School, but with need for more places for girls and increased provision for boys in Shrewsbury, the tradition came to an end.

Problems created by the Second World War also brought to an end at SHS another characteristic feature of many Trust schools – the boarding house. Cyngfeld, Kingsland, was the last and largest of several houses used for this purpose and had flourished since 1920. There were probably never more than about forty boarders at any one time, but it must have solved problems for many parents and girls, and fond memories are treasured of the way of life it provided.

In 1958 the Council decided to increase the numbers in the upper school by introducing a two-form entry. Hitherto 'little Shrewsbury' had been much the smallest of the Trust schools but now the need for a wider choice in the curriculum demanded larger numbers in the middle school and sixth form, to make the provision economic. Though the Trust had provided a proportion of free places since 1911, the larger numbers envisaged in the direct grant arrangements of 1944 made further expansion desirable.

In 1959 Hampden House, vacated by the junior school, became the geography room and art studios – with the basement adapted for pottery

in 1971 – and shortly afterwards, No. 28 Town Walls was purchased and became the music school. Two fine modern laboratories for physics and chemistry were opened in 1961 and it is hoped that before long a new block may make it possible to concentrate all science facilities in one area.

In common with grammar schools all over the country, the school was experiencing by the mid sixties a steady rise in sixth-form numbers and a consequent need for diversity in patterns of sixth-form courses. New courses at universities and polytechnics encouraged new combinations of subjects to be studied to Advanced Level, creating in turn fresh possibilities for girls with no particular subject requirements to pursue lines of study which interested them. This period saw the disappearance of prefects and the special privileges and status associated with that minute but treasured prefects' room, the departure from the house system, and in 1970 the replacement of upper and lower sixth forms by tutor groups in which the different generations and disciplines mingle. All sixth-formers continue to help on a voluntary basis with the running of the school and many make valuable contributions to its life.

In 1967 the Trust bought Crescent Lane House and parents, friends, and old girls raised £1,500 to help with its conversion and furnishing. The house, with its pleasant atmosphere and remoteness from the main building, lends itself happily to sixth-form occupation – though those who plod up and down the garden in snow or with umbrellas may have reservations about this! The first visitor entertained there to tea was the Patron, HRH the Duchess of Gloucester, who very kindly elected to visit the school on a sunny day in July 1968 when she was in Shrewsbury to open a new hospital.

Shrewsbury: Visit of HRH THE DUCHESS OF GLOUCESTER (on right)

Besides the sixth-form common-room and study, the house affords space for French conversation, a room where dressmaking and creative embroidery can be taught to small groups, a small staff room, and the Walker Room, generously furnished with a grant from the Walker Trust, where, in a rather confined space, French is taught with audio-visual aids.

Now in its eighty-seventh year, Shrewsbury has 574 pupils, 184 in the junior school and 390 in the senior school, of whom 91 are in the sixth form. Less highly selective and distinguished academically nowadays than its sisters in more populous areas, the school continues to pursue its course with happy zest and unabated spirit. Future developments already planned include a new hall/gymnasium, a second laboratory block, and a new set of classrooms on the site of the present canteen kitchen, which will be replaced by new premises elsewhere. In the main building we plan for the enlargement of the library and the study areas which should surround it. There is much to be accomplished in the next decade and we are eager to set about it.

South Hampstead

MRS S. WILTSHIRE, BSC

'The highest school in London' – thus the Marquis of Lorne described South Hampstead High School twenty-one years after its foundation in 1876. He was, perhaps, urging its members to aim high and maintain their reputation for a high standard of scholarship – the school in actual fact is perched on the edge of a hillside well below the level of Hampstead's famous heath.

South Hampstead, the tenth school to be founded, opened at a house in Winchester Road, North London, under the name of St John's Wood High School. Only 27 pupils assembled on the first day, but in two years the number had increased to 197. Six years later there were 302 pupils on the roll, and early reminiscences speak of the necessity to carry on three classes in one room (divided from each other by curtains), so that it was possible to hear 'at least two of the teachers, but neither very distinctly'. Clearly, it was necessary to provide larger premises, and the present school in Maresfield Gardens (designed by the father of one of the first pupils) was opened by the Princess Louise in 1882.

South Hampstead is one of the most 'urban' of the Trust's schools. Its catchment area is wide, covering a large part of North and West London, but the prevailing influence is undoubtedly that of Hampstead itself, a cosmopolitan and artistic society, with a long tradition as an asylum for political and other refugees. Perhaps it is significant that South Hampstead is the only school in the Trust to have adopted a German motto, 'Mehr Licht'. It has always been strongly supported by the Jewish community. All this variety helps to create a lively intellectual atmosphere combined with breadth of interests. It may also account for the strong emphasis on individuality, a daily reminder of which is given by the sixth-form girls who, no longer in uniform, display 'ensembles' for every taste.

It is said that there was a moment in the school's early history when it was 'in a bad way'. Its rescuer, and headmistress from 1886 to 1918, was Miss M. S. Benton, one of the most commanding of the many great personalities who have served the Trust. Another whose wisdom over twenty-six years guided the school through one of its most formative periods, including the vicissitudes of wartime evacuation and reconstruction, was Miss M. L. Potter, a scholar imbued with imaginative insight into the needs of individuals and moved by a quiet kindness and humanity which have left a lasting impression. Her successor, Miss P. R. Bodington, who came to South Hampstead from the headship of Norwich, steered the school 'with gentleness and wisdom' along ways congenial to its always forward-looking nature. When she came to retire in 1969, the school magazine, in its characteristically contemporary fashion, drew out the highlights of her very distinguished career by means of an interview.

· Among those highlights, from South Hampstead's point of view, must be counted the acquisition of a site adjoining the school on which a bungalow then stood. In a district in which space and land are at a premium this was an achievement indeed. With the help of parents and the Trust a large, well-equipped science building has been built. It was opened in March 1971 by Professor Dorothy Hodgkin, the Nobel Laureate, and is proving a stimulus to science teaching in the school. The number of girls taking science subjects in the upper forms seems to be increasing already, and the Nuffield Combined Science Course is being introduced in the middle school. The space liberated by the coming of the new laboratories is fully utilized, but even so activities spill over into odd corners. The first impression on visitors seems to be one of bustle and pace, and to fit the girls' varied interests and enthusiasms into such a compact school means complex schedules and time-tables. The new building, however, has made it possible to take a less cluttered view of the more eligible parts of the old: for example the fine house adjoining the playground (acquired in 1921) which was once the residence of Sir Ernest Waterlow, whose beautiful studio has been a great asset to the school.

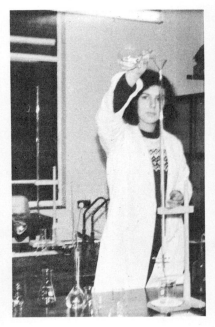

Another development remarked on by Miss Bodington, the growth in sixth-form numbers, also continues, and some newcomers join the school at this stage. In keeping with the times, the girls are increasingly involved in school affairs. There is a School Council in which they can voice their opinions, and they have now largely taken responsibility for such school 'traditions' as the magazine, which they edit and produce; they also contribute imaginatively to such institutions as the daily assembly.

The school's strong sense of community and social service is still upheld through work with the aged and handicapped. In the causes chosen for financial support there is again a note of originality: the enthusiasm which led pupils of 1911 to subscribe towards the cost of two dogs in Scott's antarctic expedition, which resulted in a portrait of Captain Scott being sent to the school by Commander Evans, had its more recent counterpart in 1956 when the school became the supporter of a husky name Jo, in the antarctic expedition of that year. A few years ago one form bought a cow for a farmer whose livelihood was threatened by a foot and mouth epidemic.

Though we have no playing fields, and the girls have to go to Regent's Park in coaches, we still sometimes produce a member of a county hockey eleven; and sometimes we win the Trust netball rally. Fencing – a recent introduction – has a rapidly expanding following, both as a club activity throughout the school and as part of the sixth-form curriculum; some of our judo enthusiasts have gained 'belts' of various colours, and we all enjoy the grace of the interpretive dancing.

We have always been very strong in music, art, and drama. There are senior and junior orchestras, large choirs, and numerous ensembles and trios for strings, wind, and brass, and we find ourselves involved in many outside musical activities as well. A substantial number of girls go on to art schools every year, and examples of their work are sought for many local exhibitions. The school play is a feature of the Christmas term; and during the biennial summer drama festivals, when plays chosen, produced, and acted by each senior form are judged by an outside adjudicator, everything else seems to stop!

At her last prizegiving Miss Potter said she always hoped that South Hampstead girls would turn out to be 'worthwhile partners in any enterprise'. The articulate young women of today, with their distinctive hairstyles and fashions and original opinions on all current social issues, through their practical and spontaneous concern, offer their partnership to the suffering and underprivileged, and bridge whatever gaps may exist between the generations.

South Hampstead: '. . . a large, well-equipped science building.'

Streatham Hill

THEN AND NOW—MUSIC

Ipswich

Streatham Hill & Clapham

MISS I. A. WULFF, BA

Streatham Hill High School opened in 1887 as Brixton Hill High School in a large house on Brixton Hill, No. 260. There were nine pupils from five families, four of whom had left by 1891 on account of 'ill health'. Against all the others, under the heading 'Reasons for leaving' is listed: 'Finished her education.' The professions of the parents are given as 'Slate merchant', 'Surveyor and Auctioneer', 'Cloth Agent', and, rather mysteriously, 'No profession'. Another register lists 'Father's profession' in all cases as 'Gentleman'.

The headmistress was Miss Alice Tovey. In 1892 Miss Reta Oldham was appointed as an assistant mistress, and upon Miss Tovey's retirement in 1898 she became headmistress, continuing until 1923; in 1917 she was elected for two years as President of the Association of Head Mistresses, a distinction shared by her successor, Miss G. R. Gwatkin, in 1935.

In 1894 the school had outgrown the premises in Brixton Hill and a new school was built at Streatham Hill. This was formally opened by Princess Louise in 1895. Early photographs of the building show that it stood alone in fields, and presented an imposing façade to Wavertree Road. It still has one of the finest views in London; from the third floor one can see St Paul's cathedral, the Post Office tower, and indeed most of the spires, towers, and office blocks of importance, as well as Hampstead Heath, and in the other direction, Epsom Downs. At one side of the building was a large elm tree, remembered affectionately by the girls of many generations, though it has now given way to the spacious library, the geography room, and the biology laboratory.

Not far away was the wide road, Palace Road, constructed to lead from London to the great Crystal Palace Exhibition in 1851. This road was lined with large houses of dignity and gracious proportions, one of which was purchased in 1938, to contain first the Clapham & Streatham Hill Training College, and afterwards the junior school, which has remained there. The possession of a large garden is highly prized by the school which of all the Trust's schools is nearest to central London.

In the main school, old girls of the period before the Second World War remember particularly the assembly hall with a 'modelled and painted frieze' by Mr Matthew Webb, and a huge statue of the Venus de Milo presented by the girls on the school's twenty-first birthday. There was an organ given by Miss Tovey, the first headmistress, a grand piano, and a beaten copper shield with the motto 'Keep Faith', given by the staff. Later the old girls purchased the grounds of an adjoining tennis club and presented these to the school, so that although the surrounding fields of former days are now the sites of numerous houses, the school retains quite a large open space in its immediate vicinity, every inch of which is used either for tennis and netball courts or for gardens and lawns, very important now that the majority of the pupils are flat dwellers.

One of the first girls to go to university was Ida Baumann, who entered Royal Holloway College in 1894. The numbers who went on to further training and to take degrees were small in those days, but Holloway and Westfield were favourite choices, and in the twenties Newnham received several Streatham scholars, amongst them the future Dame Beryl Paston Brown, who became head of Homerton College of Education.

In 1938 the school was amalgamated with the academically distinguished Clapham High School under Miss Marjorie Jarrett, to form the present Streatham Hill & Clapham High School. In 1931 Miss Winifred Hartwell was appointed senior mathematics mistress, and since she continued to lead the mathematics department and was later also senior mistress until her retirement in 1962, she established a particular interest, already begun under Miss Gwatkin, in this subject, which has continued to flourish.

The Second World War caused some division, though in spirit the school emerged more united than ever after facing and sharing many difficulties. There was some evacuation to Brighton, where the Trust school received Streatham girls and staff kindly; when Brighton turned out to be as dangerous as London, some girls went to Guildford, some elected to return to Streatham, and still others went to Halifax in parties of twenty at a time. The younger staff spent many nights fire-watching, and most lessons took place in the shelters.

On 27 July 1944 most of the main school was destroyed by a flying bomb, but work was carried on gallantly in various local houses until the rebuilding after the war and the formal opening of the new school by the Duchess of Gloucester on 22 October 1952. The building is compact and solid, and those of a new generation who find it somewhat uncompromising in appearance may be reminded by the following lines, written by an old girl in the twenties, that beauty is in the eye of the beholder:

> 'O rose red walls, long years have sped
>   Since first you sheltered me. I tread
> Once more the well worn ways where spread
>   The elm tree's lofty boughs . . .'

In 1947 Miss Margaret Macaulay was appointed to succeed Miss Jarrett in the difficult task of keeping the routine going until rebuilding was completed. She continued the tradition of scholarship in classics fostered by Miss Gwatkin, and in her time several girls gained not only distinction in Latin and Greek but also a lively appreciation of classical culture.

Quite early a house system dividing the school into four houses each named after a patron saint, St George, St Andrew, St David, and St Patrick, was established, and this has continued as the basis for games competitions and an annual dramatic competition in which sixth-formers produce and younger girls act. A sixth-form society was formed after the Second World War with two other girls' schools and three boys' schools in the South London area, and this meets five times a year for lectures, music, social functions, and so on.

The school today has 478 pupils. Nearly all leavers go on to further training of some kind, to universities and degree and diploma courses in many types of institution. In the last twenty years girls have become doctors, artists, musicians, nurses, lawyers, journalists, novelists, teachers, secretaries, accountants, social workers, pharmacists, and physio-therapists, to mention only a few.

Facilities have been extended, and in addition to laboratories for all sciences, a small language room houses tape recorders and record players with which girls can themselves practise French, German, Spanish, or Russian. Mrs Clara Slee, née Baumann, who was a sister of Ida Baumann mentioned above, was an early pupil gifted in languages, and became the first woman interpreter in the Secretariat of the League of Nations. She would have been pleased to know, had she lived, that the school won in 1970 the prize for French and German Verse-speaking, awarded in competition with schools in London, the Home Counties, and East Anglia, by the Modern Languages Association.

Girls still play the organ, and there is quite a large choir and an orchestra. The school is connected to the ILEA Closed Circuit Television, and naturally also makes use of the national television network. Though the girls again play hockey on Clapham Common as they did in the early years, there is a hockey field; the assembly hall with the frieze has turned into a gymnasium with space for judo and badminton, as well as up-to-date physical education apparatus, whilst a new hall with a stage for acting was added in 1952. There is a great interest in drama, and anyone staging a play has difficulty in booking the hall for rehearsals: at the time of writing four house plays, four middle school scenes from Shakespeare, one lower sixth play (Strindberg's *Easter*), and a modern dance version of *The Ancient Mariner* are in production.

There are modern facilities for cooking and sewing, and it is the only Trust school to have a sixth-form secretarial course with up-to-date office equipment. This and the many projectors for films and slides, the calculating machine, the overhead projector, and so on, are separated by eighty-five years from the humble beginning in which the inventory lists one hat and coat stand, a coal scuttle, fifteen pairs of dumb-bells, and the simplest necessities such as chairs and tables.

There are two natural advantages that have developed with time: the first is the proximity to London with the increasing opportunities to visit concerts, galleries, museums, exhibitions, and conferences; the second is the richness of different cultures and backgrounds, now that girls from many parts of the world attend the school and mix and learn from each other. Amongst them there are perhaps fifteen or more languages spoken. At Christmas this resulted in a beautiful Nativity celebration in many different languages and incorporating international customs and traditions. Such a school seems a suitable place in which to be educated for life in a multiracial society.

Sutton

MISS J. R. GLOVER, MA

Like the other Trust schools, Sutton's original home was in a family house, which still forms a main part of our ever-increasing network of buildings, and all our visitors and parents approach our community up the flight of stone steps, with its friendly archway of cotoneaster, through the original front door, which bears the notice we all think could form the motto of the GPDST: 'This door opens outwards.'

Our door always has opened outwards. Miss M. C. Whyte, our first headmistress, was gifted with musical and artistic talent, and she also possessed the blessed quality of seeing education as a process which should stimulate width of interest and correlation of studies, so that while she was determined that Sutton girls should enjoy academic work and develop scholarly judgement, she also insisted that music, art, and literature should form the basis of all else. Miss Whyte started with eighty pupils on 17 January 1884, and within fifteen months some of them were writing Oxford Local Examinations. By 1886, this dynamic and purposeful head-mistress had expanded the school so much that a dining room, assembly hall, studio, and five new classrooms had been built. This assembly hall later became the gymnasium and is still used as such, and the dining room, originally designed for about a hundred people, saw Sutton through its lunch hours until January 1972, when at last it was superseded by the much more ample accommodation we now enjoy.

From the earliest years Sutton has lived in family homes, which the Council has bought one by one, adding the needed provision for the expanding interests and increasing numbers of girls and staff: these houses and their gardens have formed a framework within which purpose-built additions have been fitted, notably the beautiful hall and fine library, both completed just before the Second World War, the splendid Lilian Charles-worth room which was opened in 1959, and much more recently, in 1971, the three-storeyed building behind Suffolk House, with its five classrooms and seven laboratories, and the swimming pool, given by the generosity of parents, friends, and old girls, to be used for the first time in summer 1972. In common with our sister schools, we enjoy the privilege of having our own junior department, and the activities and personalities of the younger children, from the kindergarten upwards, provide an additional factor which makes for a family feeling. Sutton girls derive a lot of pleasure from the homely, odd corners of the older buildings and the areas of garden and lawns that we still retain, and they also find the junior school a most humanizing influence. When I came to Sutton in 1959, I was touched and impressed and also much relieved to recognize at once an atmosphere in which individuals were known and understood and expected to develop

in their own way, without being subjected to institutionalized arrangements, even though by then Miss Whyte's roll of 80 had lengthened to Miss Charlesworth's 900.

The *Sutton High School Chronicle*, dated 1896-9, has on its front page the school motto: 'Fortiter, Fideliter, Feliciter', and then a quotation from the poet Browning: 'The common problem – yours, mine, everyone's – is, not to fancy what were fair in Life provided it could be; but, finding first what may be, then find how to make it fair.' Together with the front door's message, these words offer a very moving interpretation of much that has been consistent in the school's life, forming its traditions and its atmosphere, and our great hope is that while our community continues to expand and to adjust to social and educational change, we shall keep the spirit which has been our mainstay during all the decades since 1884.

From the very earliest years, the girls were working for the wider community, and combining their concern for other people with their own delight in drama, music, travel, and art. The year 1888 saw one of our first dramatic productions, *She Stoops to Conquer*, performed to raise money for the Sutton Parish Sick Nursing Fund. During the nineties, parties of girls were taken to visit Cambridge and Oxford, Holland, Paris, and Brittany. Since these early days, under the guidance of Miss Whyte's four successors – Miss J. F. Duirs (1890-1903), Miss M. K. Bell (1903-23), Miss E. M. L. Lees (1923-39), and Miss L. E. Charlesworth, CBE (1939-59) – the school has always been guided to look beyond its own immediate concerns and interests. The record of domestic and foreign travel, pen friendships, exchanges, and of welcoming guests and visitors of varying ages and nationalities is much too long to set out in detail here. Concern about international affairs and especially world peace and all the movements devised to develop understanding across national frontiers has been central in the school's life and was especially promoted by Miss Charlesworth's active association with UNESCO and other international organizations.

Practical social work in the borough has become one of our biggest projects, supported by a very high proportion of our senior girls; it is linked with integrated courses planned for the upper fourths, for the Ordinary and Advanced level years, and for the general studies programmes of the sixth forms. As well as concentrating on local hospitals, welfare work, Red Cross clubs, housing schemes, and individuals in special need, this social service reaches out as far as Tibet, Uganda, Kumi, Penang, and Chabua, and helps to give point and purpose to much of our academic work.

We achieved one of our first open awards in 1897, when Frances M. West went to Somerville, and since then we have had an annual exodus from the sixth to universities, colleges of education, and to medical, art, and music schools; an analysis of the courses followed would cover a large number of disciplines, including some which are in general supposed to be difficult for women, such as aeronautics and engineering. This tradition we hold in common with the other Trust schools, and it is of course in keeping with the purposes of our founders. Equally consistent with their ideals is the steady flow of our girls into so many other professions, nursing in particular, but also all the branches of social work, librarianship, journalism, the hospital therapies, business studies and dietetics.

From the eighteen nineties onwards we have records of girls' successes in dress design courses, and especially since Miss Charlesworth's appointment, we have had a thriving home economics department, which enables many of our seniors to study not only practical cookery, but also nutrition and sociology. The art department has encouraged work in new media and includes in its schemes pottery, weaving, calligraphy, and jewellery-making. Chamber music and orchestral work appear in the account of 1897, and with other forms of music, choral and instrumental, have thrived here ever since.

Miss Whyte was quickly off the mark with regard to sport, so that the first tennis court was marked out on the front lawn by a party of girls with brushes and buckets of whitewash within months of her arrival, soon to be followed by provision for hockey, cricket, and netball. In recent years, fencing, badminton, swimming, judo, and golf have been added to the list, along with athletics.

It is not possible to record here even a summary of the outstanding turning-points in the school's history, many of which are vividly set out in *A School Remembers*, published in 1964, but one period we must never allow to diminish in memory, and that is the time of the Second World War, when Sutton experienced life and work in the air raid shelters. Miss Charlesworth's exuberant optimism, gaiety, and personal courage impressed people then perhaps more poignantly than at any other time, and the school's triumphant survival of those acutely taxing years was of course due primarily to her. The stories are legion, and some are included in the short but very revealing book.

In wartime and peacetime, Sutton girls have evolved a notable array of informal activities, run by seniors with the help of staff. Some clubs have been christened with quite extraordinary names: Braille, Debating, Sketching, Guitar, Drama, Madrigals, Stamps, Chess, Bridge, Cookery, Archaeology, and Modern Languages need no explanation, but what about the Kyrle, Phoenix, Ichthys, Forum, and Psammead Societies? All these have flourished, and doubtless more will develop in the next decade. Along with the annual sixth form Christmas concert, which nowadays raises well over £200 each time for charities, these clubs serve to draw different age groups together and to promote lasting friendships and also lasting leisure time interests. Decision making, and its consequent executive action, has in recent years been further developed, by the girls and staff, through the School Meeting, which assembles its representatives several times a term to discuss our affairs with amiable if critical and certainly detailed attention.

The Parent Staff Association was founded by Miss Charlesworth in 1946, and it has been of incalculable help to us ever since, giving very varied opportunities for parents to become involved in our projects and policies. Like the Old Girls' Association, which is of much earlier date, it has also provided us with a network of friends whose generosity in terms of financial and other gifts has been matched by the great encouragement we derive from the interest and understanding shown to us as we adjust to the ever-changing world in which we live.

So the door has opened outwards over the years, and with courage, faith, and cheerfulness we hope to meet the challenge which awaits us now, the common problems, yours, mine, everyone's.

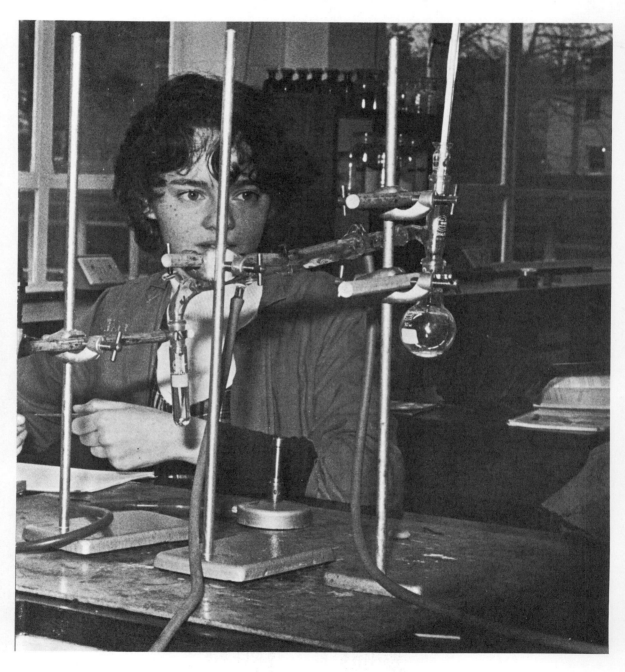

Sydenham

MISS M. I. J. HAMILTON, BA

Sydenham, affluent victorian suburb with its massive houses set in ample grounds, its Crystal Palace, centre for musicians, its space and air, must have seemed a comparative oasis in February 1887, when the High School came into being. That there ever was a Sydenham High School we owe to a Mr Chadwick, who moved from North London, where his daughter had attended the Trust school at Highbury, to the new suburb of Sydenham, and found no nearer school than Dulwich. A member of the Probate Department of Somerset House, he spoke of his difficulty to his junior, the Honourable Conrad Dillon, nephew to Lady Stanley of Alderley. She replied: 'I brought the wants of Sydenham before the Council of the GPDS Company yesterday and I think if a number of influential people, joined in a committee, were to ask for a school, the request would be entertained and the amount of shares arranged. There are two prominent questions – premises at a fair rent and plenty of girls.' Both conditions were met and the school was advertised in the parish magazine: 'The aim of the Company, which has by now 32 schools, is by the employment of an ample staff of competent teachers and the use of the best methods of instruction to ensure for girls an education adapted to their requirements but as sound and thorough as that which boys now receive in grammar schools of the highest class.' Fees ranged from three to five guineas a term.

On 22 February 1887, Sydenham High School opened its doors – at No. 72 West (now Westwood) Hill, formerly a hotel – to its first twenty pupils, three more than were expected. They were welcomed by Miss Irene Thomas, the first headmistress, and two members of staff. The school grew rapidly, and in three years numbered 237. An adjoining house, Fairlight, was bought and an assembly hall built, opened in 1891 by the Princess Louise, who insisted on visiting every formroom and, sitting at one of the desks, pronounced it 'very comfortable'. The rapid growth of the school was largely attributed to the personality of Miss Thomas, who resigned because of ill health in 1901. Her phenomenal memory, her celtic temperament, so quick but so tactful that, as one parent put it, 'Miss Thomas is the only person I know who can put the fat in the fire and draw it out again', were the qualities that launched the school.

Miss Sheldon succeeded her, establishing the good standards of academic work already set, and lively work throughout the school was spoken of, not simply that of the most brilliant. There were many innovations: a home arts department was opened; the library began, expanding from a cupboard to a bookcase, then to a room; the orchestra was formed; games were organized as club activities, hockey being the most popular, aided by a tram as a peripatetic pavilion from whose top younger members could watch matches; the houses, Grey, Gurney, Louise, and Stanley were established; and the first magazine appeared, recording familiar comments such as: 'Our form do fairly good work, leaving as our mothers say a margin for improvement', and: 'Nothing much has happened this term as our minds are engrossed by the approaching examinations.'

This was a period of consolidation, and Miss Sanders, who followed Miss Sheldon in 1917, wished for an 'education as wide as possible in scope and as varied as possible in method'. Art and music were emphasized and a large number of clubs came into existence, including a Political Society and a Literary and Dramatic Club. We read too: 'In school discipline there was an advance towards greater freedom and liberty – a matter of attitude rather than regulation – and girls responded by shewing a greater self-control and higher sense of responsibility and increased friendliness.'

The conversion of an hotel into a school had been a great success. Initially only the front rooms had been used but gradually every possible space was filled to capacity, even what was called 'the dungeon', formerly the site of the turkish bath. The conservatory became the laboratory, the assembly hall was built on the only playground, once the courtyard, and the coal was stored in the wine cellar. To Miss Sheldon, probably Sydenham's greatest benefactor, the school owed many amenities: furnishing for the first library, a grand piano, the gift of two adjoining houses in Longton Grove, an interest-free loan to buy the first tennis courts, and half the cost of the present assembly hall.

However, by 1931 when Miss Smith (Dr Smith by right, though she would not be called this) came to Sydenham, the school buildings, though possessing 'an individuality and charm which is peculiarly their own' were clearly not entirely convenient. There was no room for expansion and the lease was due to expire in 1936. Horner Grange, a house opposite, with a ballroom capable of becoming a gymnasium and a garden big enough for a hockey field, was acquired in its place and the school moved on 26 April 1934, filing across the road to take possession. By the time of the golden jubilee in 1937 the school had purpose-built laboratories, studio, classrooms, and a new hall.

While the First World War made little direct impact upon the school, the Second affected Sydenham deeply. Evacuated to Brighton in 1939, the school returned to Sydenham in 1940, to face flying bombs and rockets. When Miss Smith left in 1941 for the headship of King Edward VI High School, Birmingham, there were only 87 girls in the school, and so it was when Miss Yardley succeeded her as headmistress. Numbers rose again until the flying bomb attacks, during which public examinations had to be taken in the cloakroom, forced a temporary closure. Soon after the reopening, a V2 burst overhead one Thursday morning while the school was in session and descended in a thousand parts on roof and grounds. The school was fortunate indeed to escape destruction and to be able to look forward, after the difficult war years, to a period of rapid expansion.

In 1949 the school became two stream and sixth-form numbers grew. The junior school was transferred to separate premises, the stable block was converted into domestic science and craft rooms, the library was enlarged. Pressure on sixth-form accommodation was relieved first by two caravans, which aroused much comment, and then by a Swift-Plan annexe. In 1958 a building fund for urgently needed laboratory space was launched: generously supported by parents, pupils, and friends, it provided about £5,500 towards the cost of the new science and geography wing, opened in 1965.

In 1966, when Miss Yardley retired, the school had weathered the storms of war, grown to 550 pupils, increased and improved its accommodation, and above all had re-established a rich and flexible community life.

As the suburb of Sydenham itself has changed, with great houses yielding place to smaller, and motor traffic flowing down Westwood Hill, once thought too steep for a bus service, so has the school. But whatever the changes, essences remain: the maintenance of good academic standards, whether in arts or sciences, where numbers increase yearly; the interest in music and creative art; the enjoyment of club activities, fluctuating with changes in fashion – chess last year, bridge this; the house system, with its increasing work for good causes, in particular the Union of Girls' Schools Settlement in Peckham; the interest and help of parents and old girls. Outwardly, however, there have been changes: in buildings, in sixth-form apparel and organization, in the introduction of audio-visual equipment, and in the arrival of coffee machines, communal telephone, and snack lunches.

As we stand beside the fire burning beneath the great copper canopy, the glory of the entrance hall, and contemplate the expansion of the junior school into an additional building and the effort required to obtain the new gymnasium/hall and sixth-form block, for which we now hope, the coals seem no less bright, despite the necessity for smokeless fuel, for they seem to symbolize the strength which lies in the union of past and present.

Wimbledon

MRS A. A. PIPER, MA

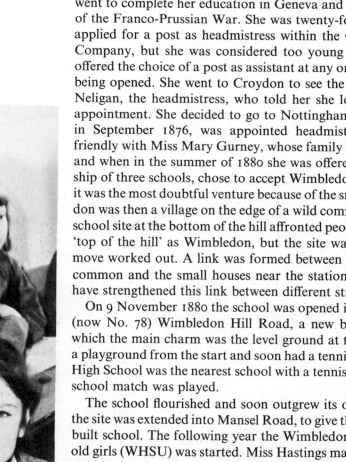

Miss Hastings was the first headmistress of Wimbledon High School when she was only twenty-nine. Her precocity in teaching herself to read by the time she was three was possibly a foretaste of her youthful appointment. She was educated at home until she was sixteen when she went as a boarder to a school in Richmond where she studied French and German. She then went to complete her education in Geneva and was there at the outbreak of the Franco-Prussian War. She was twenty-four in 1875 when she first applied for a post as headmistress within the Girls' Public Day School Company, but she was considered too young for a headship, and was offered the choice of a post as assistant at any one of the four new schools being opened. She went to Croydon to see the school and to meet Miss Neligan, the headmistress, who told her she looked too young for *any* appointment. She decided to go to Nottingham High School, and later, in September 1876, was appointed headmistress. There she became friendly with Miss Mary Gurney, whose family home was in Wimbledon, and when in the summer of 1880 she was offered the choice of the headship of three schools, chose to accept Wimbledon, despite a warning that it was the most doubtful venture because of the small population. Wimbledon was then a village on the edge of a wild common and the choice of the school site at the bottom of the hill affronted people who accepted only the 'top of the hill' as Wimbledon, but the site was chosen – and this bold move worked out. A link was formed between the big houses round the common and the small houses near the station. Succeeding generations have strengthened this link between different strata of society.

On 9 November 1880 the school was opened in its first home at No. 74 (now No. 78) Wimbledon Hill Road, a new but unfurnished house of which the main charm was the level ground at the back. The school had a playground from the start and soon had a tennis court laid out. Croydon High School was the nearest school with a tennis court, and the first inter-school match was played.

The school flourished and soon outgrew its original building. In 1887 the site was extended into Mansel Road, to give the older pupils a purpose-built school. The following year the Wimbledon High School Union for old girls (WHSU) was started. Miss Hastings maintained her contact with past pupils with a lively interest in all the 'Circles', French, English, Music, and Dramatic into which the Wimbledon High School Union was divided. She asked all the members to complete each year a record giving (1) the names and authors of all the books that they had read, (2) an account of how they had spent their money, (3) details of the manual work that they had done. This habit, inculcated when young, remained with many old girls throughout their lives, and if we could find them these returns would be most interesting!

The love of learning was encouraged for its own sake. Miss Hastings refused to give prizes and said that public examinations, far from being the be-all and end-all of a girl's school life, should be regarded as strictly incidental to the real purpose of education and taken with a light heart.

A pupil who left in 1908 – the year Miss Hastings retired – wrote in 1930: 'My generation was more fortunate than the present in the stability of its life and outlook. We mostly stayed in one place, had one background of home and school through our growing years. How great, then, was the influence of that school! Some will remember one thing most clearly, some another. For me, the intense interest of work emerges, and a gallery of faces, interesting people, mistresses and girls, but behind this shifting panorama was one quiet strong personality that did not change.'

Miss Gavin succeeded Miss Hastings and continued as headmistress until her death in 1918. The heavy war years took their toll. In February 1917, when the school was burnt down, Miss Gavin was in bed seriously ill with bronchitis. A loud explosion in the early morning was first thought to be a Zeppelin raid, but flames shooting up from the roof of the main school indicated a fire. The alarm was given, but the fire engine from Wandsworth took forty minutes to come; it was the darkest night of the year and a late snowfall followed by frost had made the roads slippery. Meanwhile the school's own firefighting equipment was used but was incapable of controlling the blaze, and there were difficulties about cutting off the gas supply.

The fire destroyed the whole of the main school building, and Miss Hastings was asked to help Miss Gavin with the immediate problems of rehousing. Within three weeks the school had settled into houses in Grosvenor Hill and Ridgway Place, and by using every available corner of the preparatory house, life proceeded reasonably normally.

Miss Lewis, who was appointed headmistress in September 1918, worked hard over the trials of rebuilding and when, in October 1920, the rebuilt school was formally opened by the Duchess of Atholl (an old girl) the house at the corner (now Nos. 74/76 Wimbledon Hill Road) had been taken over for the junior school. The outside walls of the main building on Mansel Road had been left standing and were re-used. With adjustments to a staircase it was possible to enlarge the studio, incorporate a gymnasium and science block, and rebuild the library, with a dignified fireplace as a memorial to Miss Gavin.

In July 1923 the Parents' Committee, under the chairmanship of Mr Edwardes-Jones, asked the Council to negotiate the purchase of the former grounds of the All-England Lawn Tennis Club. The parents were prepared to give practical support: they decided to make a maintenance subscription of five shillings for each child, and, in addition, subscribed for debentures issued by the Trust which gave an interest-free loan of £2,000. In this way, the required £6,000 was raised.

The old centre court is part of the present hockey pitch. The diamond jubilee of the All-England Lawn Tennis Club and the silver jubilee of

King George V fell in 1935 and it seemed fitting that a dual jubilee commemoration appeal be launched. By then, the school had, through its own efforts, raised enough to pay off the Trust loan and the debenture holders; and the jubilee appeal completed the playing fields by providing, among other things, the handsome commemoration gates formally opened in May of that year.

The outstanding event which took place during Miss Lewis's headship – possibly the greatest contribution made by Wimbledon High School to the Trust – was the 'Battle of Wimbledon High School'. Since the early nineteenth century, boys' Public Schools had enjoyed exemption from tax in respect of school buildings, but no girls' High School had ever claimed it. In 1925 the battle started and it was only on 29 July 1930 that judgement was given in the House of Lords in favour of the school. Mr Edwardes-Jones, KC (he had daughters at the school), worked extremely hard throughout these five years. He wrote in 1930: 'The success of the case was primarily due to the wonderful record and position of the school itself but a contributory cause was the fact that every lady member of the Council was throughout in favour of fighting the fight to a finish.'

The decision in the case of Wimbledon High School applied to all the schools of the Trust and to many others. It brought Wimbledon High School a substantial sum of money in repayment of tax, and this money enabled the Council to purchase for the school, in April 1931, an acre of the grounds of the Draxmont Estate.

During Miss Lewis's years at Wimbledon the numbers at school rose from 300 to over 500 and it was sad that after the Second World War had begun, in her last term, the numbers dropped dramatically.

Miss Littlewood came from the headship of Bromley to Wimbledon in January 1940 and had to deal with all the problems of reduced numbers (and redundant staff) as well as other wartime difficulties. The basements were not built for housing the remaining classes – seven or eight of them at once! Miss Littlewood's leadership, however, enabled the school to carry on, if not quite 'as usual'. She fostered the spirit of adventure, and with it the warmth of fellowship. Her courage and gaiety held the school together under all difficulties.

The staff and the older girls took turns fire-watching and everyone joined in 'digging for victory'. The fire-watchers had to cope with several incidents. On the night of 7 November 1940 (two days before the school's sixtieth birthday) nine bombs fell in the grounds, broke most of the windows and brought down several ceilings. Lessons next day, hardly as usual, were given in the dining rooms and cloakrooms while volunteer parties cleared up the debris. The birthday celebrations for the next day were necessarily postponed but at least the girls were back in their formrooms. With transport frequently dislocated the girls and staff often arrived late or not at all – and sometimes despaired of getting home. Then the cloakroom became a dormitory.

The 'doodle bugs' of 1944 brought increasing strain. Although our numbers had fallen the public examination candidates filled all the shelter space available so school examinations were taken at home. The final

flying bomb to fall in Wimbledon did the school more damage than anything else. The blast blew out doors and windows, destroyed floors and
ceilings, and completely wrecked the playroom and preparatory cloakroom. This happened during the summer holidays and because the
buildings were in a dreadful condition plans were again made for evacuation, and castles in Scotland were inspected. The staff, pupils, and parents,
however, set to work and the school opened – with no doors or windows –
only three weeks late. Refurbishing and painting followed.

The numbers of pupils increased after the war and went on increasing,
and Miss Burke, when she took over from Miss Littlewood in 1949,
inherited buildings which were not nearly large enough. During the fifties
building plans were made and in 1955 Miss Burke, supported by the
parents, launched a seventy-fifth birthday building fund and raised
£1,600 at a fête. This money helped to build the new hall block on the
leasehold land of which the Trust acquired the freehold in 1959. Building
continued and in January 1962 three additional new classrooms on the
upper netball court were ready for use. In that year, a bumper year for
university awards, Wimbledon High School was reported as being 'the
top girls' school in England'. This was a fitting climax to Miss Burke's
headship, another highlight of which was the first performance in 1952
of an opera, *A Statue for the Mayor*, composed by Hugo Cole especially
for the school.

There is no chance to stand still in a school. We must look forward.
Now that the first stage of our ninetieth birthday appeal is finished we can
review what has been achieved and look forward to stage two. Our heart-
warming initial success has enabled us to buy Avon House (No. 82
Wimbledon Hill Road) complete with swimming pool. The pool has been
repaired and we are now considering plans to adapt the house itself, and
we hope to start work on a new purpose-built junior school shortly. The
Trust has most generously allocated money for a science block. The plans
are on the board and building is due to start this year.

The Crests

Bath

Birkenhead

Blackheath

Brighton & Hove

Bromley

Croydon

Ipswich

Kensington

Liverpool

Newcastle (Central)

Norwich

Nottingham

Notting Hill & Ealing

Oxford

Portsmouth

Putney

Sheffield

Shrewsbury

South Hampstead

Streatham Hill & Clapham

Sutton

Sydenham

Wimbledon

Conclusion

In 1967 the Public Schools Commission, first appointed by HM Government in 1965, was given additional terms of reference, namely: 'To advise on the most effective method or methods by which direct grant grammar schools . . . can participate in the movement towards comprehensive re-organization and to review the principle of central government grant to these schools.' During this phase of its work the Commission was under the Chairmanship of Professor David Donnison, and the report embodying its recommendations, which appeared in 1970, is commonly known as the 'Donnison report'.

The Trust hoped the Commission would be able to propose a continued partnership between the public system and the independently founded schools, such as its own, which in the course of the twentieth century have accepted the direct grant status. In submitting evidence to the Commission, the Council emphasized two great virtues of the direct grant system; the partnership between public and private control and finance, and the accessibility of basically fee-paying schools to pupils irrespective of parental income. These virtues found no favour with the Commissioners, who recommended the withholding of grant aid from any schools charging fees, and strongly urged that the existing direct grant schools be assimilated to the system of non-selective state comprehensive schools which they hoped would become universal. Had this line been followed, schools such as the Trust's would have forfeited the independent financial control which enables them to make their distinct contribution to the national and local provision, and academically orientated schools would have been available only to the very rich. With the change of government the report was shelved, and the link between the direct grant schools and the state system remains unbroken. The schools have recently been much encouraged by the introduction of arrangements to bring the fees for residuary places (assessed on an income scale) within the reach of parents of all incomes – an adjustment made urgent by changes in the value of money since the scale was first devised.

Nevertheless, there is no room for complacency. When the Donnison report was published the Council of the Trust made it clear that if the Government were to withdraw the financial support which makes possible the direct grant system, the Trust would, with the greatest reluctance, choose independence for its schools rather than their virtual extinction. We here reiterate the declaration made in 1970:

'The Council of The Girls' Public Day School Trust reaffirms its intention to carry on the work of the Trust: to provide and administer as an autonomous educational body, schools which encourage girls to develop their academic gifts within the framework of a good general education, and to go forward to the many fields of higher education now open to them.'

To conclude on a more domestic note. As will be apparent from this centenary review, the Trust's schools have grown up together over the past hundred years as members of a joint educational enterprise, to which they belong just as surely as they do to their own local communities. What that has meant to the individuals who have worked and learned in them can best be expressed in the words of one who as a young member of staff attended the jubilee thanksgiving in 1923 and hopes – intends – to be present, as a retired headmistress, at the centenary celebrations in June 1972.

'At that time, though I was very happy, enjoying my work and appreciating the school, I had no conception of the great Trust "family" or of its founders.'

The great service at St Paul's, the throng of old girls and of present pupils – a sea of 'bobbing school hats with their varied school colours' left a lifelong impression:

'From that day I belonged heart and mind to the whole family of the GPDST, its history, its present and future significance had become my great concern and within its fellowship I have found friendships which have brought some of the special joys of my life.'

The Council and Officers

March 1972